THE SINS OF THE
MOTHERS

The Legacy of Doris

D.L. SUCHAN

Table Of Contents

Fairy Tale Faith

Why do what is right, if there is nothing known to be learned?
Why do what is right when no gain is discerned?

Fairy tales are real and our life writes its stage.
If they are to exist, they must be earned.
This is how they are made.

Part 1:
The Legacy of Doris

Introduction
The Legacy of Doris

"...but what I realize is that if you don't tell your story, somebody else is writing your history." Huma Abedin[1]

Unlike Hillary Clinton's right hand, I am unlikely to be written about. What I face is invisibility. In my case, in the case of Doris, she is the only one still alive who knows the beginnings of her story. First-hand witnesses would be hard to come by.

The genetic father, the adopted father, her only sibling, her mother, her ex-husband, and all grandparents are no longer alive. As a military brat, very few and very brief contacts were made with cousins, aunts, uncles, teachers, classmates, or neighbors. Friendships, if they existed at all, were short-lived and superficial. The immediate family, as a unit of four, never attended church or any other socially organized constructs.

Abusive households tend to be isolated households. Constant moving only exacerbated the loneliness, and the feeling of exclusion. Few knew of Doris. Even fewer knew her. The two children can only bear witness to her adulthood. Doris is the bedrock of their mother.

She is initially referred to in the third person in this writing. The act of distancing encourages compassion, and I would address her needs and offer balm for her. This is meant to be a discovery—an

---

[1]https://www.cbsnews.com/news/huma-abedin-on-overcoming-betrayals-of-her-husband-anthony-weiner/

aligning of the memory, of peace. As I have aged, the need to know far outweighs any useless need for vengeance or revenge.

The lies, the betrayals, all of it needs assimilation at the very least for me. The inside, the outside, but mostly the blindside of my years from birth to the majority need to be aligned within my system. Only then do I feel that the travails of the adult can be addressed with this further, necessary clarity.

This has been a necessary trip for me. Many corners of my young world were not sufficiently understood by my young eyes, my young heart, my young and still-developing personality. The memories of the child, within the adult, remain.

What I could corroborate, I did. Some of what I could not remember was remembered by others. Some of the rememberings do not agree with me, with others. Not certain of the beginnings, I certainly did not entertain how this would end.

How many times does a child have the rug yanked out from under them and land with anything that resembles even the appearance of grace? I find myself surprised as well. It is not until you look at the accumulation of what occurred that you begin to comprehend how much damage there may be. That The Universe allows me to tell the tale, speaks volumes to her spirit, her perseverance.

Dearest Wild Thing,

I need to remember and bear witness to what has happened to you so that I may fully honor the courage of your intentions.

DLS, January 2023

Chapter 1
The Flood of 1951

17 July 1951, President Harry Truman declared a federal disaster.[2] As a son of Missouri, he knew how extensive the damage was. Four days earlier over a million acres of Kansas and close to another million acres of Missouri had flooded, leading to the deaths of seventeen people and displacing over half a million. Kansas City's Amourdale area would lose the stockyards and the flooding would see the airport moved further north to what would become The Kansas City International Airport. William McBratney was very busy.

Having served under Artillery Captain Truman in World War I, he was now a Captain of the Kansas City Fire Department. He would become the Civil Defense representative for the county. In the latter role, four years later, he would be called on to witness an atomic explosion in New Mexico. He contracted cancer of the bone from that exposure and died on the 24th of February 1957. His death certificate would read the cause to be pneumonia. At this time, he is very much alive at the age of 60, as is his wife, Lynnette, age 47.

Lynnette is also very busy. The flooding had not affected the area in which they lived and even though she knew her parents were safe; she would have been concerned for her mother's health. "Bessie" would pass a year later, but for now the American Red

---

[2] https://en.wikipedia.org/wiki/Great_Flood_of_1951
https://www.kshs.org/kansapedia/flood-of-1951/17163

Cross Grey Lady was serving her community by running a shelter facility for those displaced by the extensive flooding. She would also be concerned knowing that her eldest and only daughter was due to give birth to their first grandchild in the midst of all this chaos.

Having reached her eighth month of pregnancy and recently home from serving during the Korean Conflict, former Navy Nurse Corp Ensign Leslie Hylton would not be of much help. Luckily, Providence Hospital had also been spared.

A little over a month later, Doris Lynnette Hylton was born on the 25th of August to Leslie and her husband, James Hylton. He was not present, a fact no one found surprising. Although James still remained within the Navy, Leslie had somehow managed to be honorably discharged.

In the 1950's, Navy Nurse Corp officers do not get married without the permission of their ranking officer. Officers do not get married to enlisted men. You do not do all of the above, and then fall asleep with a Marine's baby in your arms while serving in Okinawa. Which is how the Navy discovered she was not only married to an enlisted man but pregnant with what would be the first of two children. So much for the Navy Nurse Corp. Ballard, West Virginia had not met their son's bride, so the now discharged Ensign had landed back in Kansas City, back home.

The newborn was named after the sister of James. Doris and James were not only brother and sister but good friends as well. Doris never remembered meeting her Aunt Doris, but she does remember her mother stating that she, Leslie, did not get along with her. This being so, it is something of a mystery how Doris became "Doris Lynnette."

Leslie and her mother, Lynnette, had the proverbial water and oil relationship. Even if you shook them up, they seldom presented a united front on much of anything. The daughter-mother relationship seems to have frozen into this inconsistency sometime around puberty for Leslie. In a hand-written letter that she would later write to Doris, Leslie would describe her upbringing as very stable until she became aware of boys.

Leslie spoke of studying opera and yet, apart from her mother's brief mention of this, little memory of this aspect of her mother appears to exist for Doris. There was some mention of how her West Virginian husband appreciated only The Grand Ole Opry, and after her second marriage, there would be recordings of Caruso, Irish Tenors, and others but never her mother's singing. The second husband would pretty much kill off what might have remained of her voice.

Adolescence was not a kind time for Leslie and the more Lynnette attempted to aid her, the more rebellious she became. What the mother intended as supporting, the daughter would perceive as dominating and controlling. If her daughter was concerned that she was not "popular with the boys" due to her chubbiness, Lynnette would try to help by cutting back on food consumption and increasing her physical activity.

Leslie took lessons, singing minor opera and playing tennis. All well and fine culturally but as she grew older, Lynnette would be the one to give that push to her daughter to take advantage of the opportunity to become a nurse through the Navy Nurse Corp. A Red Cross Grey Lady herself, in the late 1940s Lynnette knew that this was quite the opportunity for any young woman to advance herself. Leslie's beloved Father backed his beloved wife and off she went to become an Ensign in her early 20's.

The problem with adolescence is that it seldom has a true demarcation line. The watchful eyes of her parents and her two younger brothers were no longer present. Surrounded by people who did not know her or her family, Leslie was easily derailed. The training took 3 years and at the end of it, she would briefly serve before being released from duty. She had managed to complete three years of the Navy's nurse training, become involved with an enlisted man, secretly marry, and give birth by the age of 26.

The next few years would not be easy. Her maternal grandmother, "Bessie," will pass away a little over a year after Doris is born. She will get back to James. As she continues working as a nurse and James exits the Navy when his enlistment is up, she discovers that she is married to an alcoholic.

By April of 1954 Leslie will give birth to Loy Ray. Phoning James when she goes into labor, he will arrive just in time to see his son born. He then disappears again only to pop up four months later, whisking Leslie and the children to West Virginia. Leslie will again be working as a nurse to support the family of four when she discovers that there is another woman carrying another child by her again, absent husband. By the time her beloved Father dies on the 24th of February, a few years later, Leslie and James are divorced.

Recently widowed, Lynnette McBratney cannot stop the 2nd marriage which occurs barely a year later. Charles "Sam" Sampson miraculously shows up with a dozen roses on their doorstep. Where they initially met is unknown and was never talked about. In the household that was to be, there were seldom conversations regarding their meeting or dating. Doris does not remember any outward signs of affection between her mother and her new husband.

The 30th of June 1958, Leslie McBratney Hylton marries Charles McKinley Sampson. Two days later, after the adoption proceedings, Doris becomes Doris Lynnette Sampson and her brother, Loy Ray, becomes McKinley Charles Sampson. Anyone who understands grooming aspects can see the train wreck that is coming.

Deserted by her alcoholic father and given up for adoption, Doris is now close to the age of 7. "Mac," as he is now referred to, has recently turned 4. She is in grade school. He is just out of diapers. The new unit is now residing in Waco, Texas. Leslie is back to nursing. In a little over a year "Sam," Father-not-Father, will be sent to Alaska for a yearlong isolated tour. The remainder of the newly formed family will move to just outside James Connelly A.F.B. in Texas, to await his return.

Lynnette, Bessie, Leslie

William Leslie McBratney

Lynnette Stanley McBratney

Leslie Elizabeth McBratney

Chapter 2
Some Physical Scars

Face a world of inconsistencies, where children meant to laugh and play and grow are found crying, fearful, retreating within.

This world in which we are to be joyful in our diverse creativity becomes a dismal, constricted prison—the bars formed, ground our spirit.

A place where trust becomes an act of courage, enacted against our logic.

A place where the word "love" is often used, and the meaning always tampered with.

There was a peace she knew. A remembrance, a feeling that comes to the fore when there are butterflies or little beagle pups. She is a young one with brown hair which free-falls almost to her waist. The golden red highlights throughout its slightly unruly thickness escape all ribbons, clips, and pins. Freckles where the sun has produced them, there is no tanning for this one. She is fair. Amigo moves with her and she with him. They are friends, companions basking in the light of the day as it shifts through the wondrous, glorious trees. She remembers that day and its freedom.

The puppy is one of the things he threatens to kill. The Father-not-Father, this creator of secrets that she must not tell least the friend dies, her mother dies, her brother dies…you get the picture.

But along with these particular instances of terror, there are others that take place.

Father-not-Father is stationed in Alaska. It's an isolated tour. Doris is about the age of 9. Her mother has left to do some shopping with a friend whose husband has been kind enough to babysit the kids. She doesn't remember where the other kids have gone, but he is telling her that the Father-not-Father has told him all about her. There is no further memory save one. Later, many years later, mother will say that she fell out of a tree. There had been some bleeding.

Doris doesn't fall out of trees.

Her mother often told the tale of how she stopped striking her children. The tale speaks of a time when her little brother has angered their mother. Mother has backed the toddler into a corner and as she raises her hand to strike, Doris steps between them. Mother says that her eyes were so very sad that she never raised her hands to her children again.

Mother lies.

This is also the time period where Doris undergoes three surgeries. She has a broken eardrum. First, the tonsils go, then the first eardrum replacement is attempted, then the second finally takes. The skin grafts were taken from behind her left ear and from under her left upper arm. The scars are still there; the hearing is still impaired. All Doris remembers is her mother saying that they found a piece of aluminum foil in that left ear and no one knew how it had gotten there.

Doris doesn't put foil in her ears, or anywhere else that is inappropriate for that matter. She just ain't that kind of gal.

And the story from her mother goes… that sometime, in those early years, Doris is standing underneath the edge of a refrigerator when a glass plate of fudge falls from the top. The result is that there are several cuts on the outer edge of her right eye. They are barely visible now, camouflaged as they are with the wrinkles of time.

Doris has no comment, nor memory, to give light to this.

Chapter 3

The Last Suppers

Little boxes on a shelf,
Little boxes full of wealth,
People see but do not touch,
Little boxes made to rust.

Doris made a huge mistake while still in the Lacey Lakeview, Texas public school system. It all started out simply enough. Her grade school teacher issued an assignment. The task was to write a few paragraphs about something they really enjoyed. Doris wrote of a dish her mother made called: "Poor Man's Steak."

She did well enough in writing this piece, that her teacher overflowed with enthusiasm for her student's writing abilities. As the teacher beamed at her mother regarding the child's abilities, the mother's response was to continue to discuss the recipe and to bask in the compliments received for the dish and the child.

For the remainder of her minority, Doris would always perceive a brief and fleeting smile whenever her mother presented this dish to the family. There was no compliment given regarding her writing ability. There was no encouragement to do other than eat this dish.

Chapter 4
Divide And Isolate

The separation of mother from child. The separation of sister from brother. There is no "no man's land," no safe place or person to turn to. There are only the walls that go up, erected by the secrets that all carry. Isolated from the world and isolated from each other, none knows of the other's insults.

One of the first things that happens, when Sam forms the new family of four, is to begin the building of walls between the three. Mother-daughter-son will no longer be a unit. It wasn't difficult. Sam is not particularly smart. This unit was not very strong to begin with.

For the two siblings, the first words, first glimpses, first knowledge of their world—nurturing, came primarily from Grandmother Lynnette as Leslie was almost always working as a nurse. When Lynnette was not present, there was a void tinged with mostly passive-aggressive anger directed at them by their mother. Their alcoholic father was more absent than abusive, but Leslie could never garner enough of herself to confront him. The brother and sister were generally neglected by a woman wounded as much from her husband's behavior, as from the unstable situation she now found herself in. The solidity of the relationship was very weak when Sam began his consolidation of personal power over the individuals within this group of three.

Leslie was the first to go. The groundwork had already been laid by her first marriage, and the second male she tied herself to was even worse for her self-esteem. Wishing only to marry someone as reliable and caring as her own father, and still in the midst of mourning that father, Leslie once again had leapt into a relationship with someone who would never be the "man" she always saw her father as. Now that her mother is widowed, the last thing she wants in life is to be tied to her mother's dominion. Leslie is so resentful of her mother, that she would rather subsist on his constant devaluation of her. She seems unaware that his devaluation of her also extended to her children.

Sam expected Leslie to work outside the home. The nurse made more money than the low-ranking airman and any mention, any hint of her being aware of that, caused enough irritation that she never spoke of it. The cloak of silence in this area is so complete that it will not be until Doris is an adult, that she will realize this particular conflict in their relationship. He would demean Leslie for working outside their home, as he demanded she work outside his home.

Sam had picked his pack well. Sterile due to the mumps, his new wife brought not only additional monetary advantages, two children for him to groom, but the world would now assume he had procreated.

Imagine that you are seven years old. Your last name has changed. Your immediate family unit has changed—your grandmother is dropped, your grandfather has died, the man you once called father is nowhere to be found, and this new father is added. You've changed states and schools several times. Now, the world is telling you to refer to Loy Ray as Mac? At the age of seven, Doris has already a pretty basic understanding that the only constant in life is change.

It wasn't only the names, people and places that changed. Doris always did well in school. This was mainly due to Lynnette's early tutelage. Doris still remembers the flashcards, particularly the multiplication tables that her grandmother had used to grill her. Her numbers, her handwriting and her ability to read were all the product of her grandmother's attention to her early education.

In addition, Lynnette made dresses straight from McCall's magazine for her. If Doris could remember her first couple of years of public schooling, those would be good memories. She does not remember much. Life rather quickly turned into a reverse Cinderella story which had additional trials added.

Childhood memories are few for her. Doris remembers very, very little of her grade school days. There are no pictures to remind her. No mementos. It won't be until Junior High that she'll be remembering, that she'll be present in her memory.

I suspect part of her "checked-out," was likely disassociated. It is also highly likely that this is why she has almost no memory of her brother during this time period. What memories there are have a certain fear level, otherwise there was no childhood, few memories of her brother in her life. She had gone from fierce protection of her sibling to barely registering that he existed.

Both adults worked shifts, and it was not often that those shifts coincided. Her shifts occurred during the evening hours where she earned more. His shifts were set on a rotational basis. Days off also varied. Seldom would the couple be off at the same time, sleeping at the same time, or eating at the same time. The group of four seldom did anything as a group, and even more seldom would that activity be an outside-the-home excursion.

Even though Doris is but three years older than her little brother, it wasn't long before Doris was put in charge when both adults were absent. Those times would be the best of times for the sister and brother. The worst times were when he was home, they were not in school, and their mother was at the hospital.

For the first time in their lives, Doris and Mac have separate bedrooms. Perhaps this would not be particularly noteworthy if it were not that whenever Sam went on an isolated tour, the remaining family of three would be moved out of their present abode into one that had but two bedrooms. During isolated tours, the siblings shared a bedroom. Neither sibling knew of the sexual abuse of the other. Both thought they were the only ones receiving such attention.

Part of the method used to part mother from daughter was to set up jealousy. As Leslie would be belittled by Sam, he would throw in something positive about Doris. This would not be done in front of Doris, but she would overhear it. Additionally, periodically, Leslie would hurl a remark her way that was tinged with something that would have originally been heard by Doris from Sam.

This psyche game would be relatively easy to set up. Leslie adored her father and deeply resented her mother's closeness to him. Sam simply had only to redirect the already existing Electra-like complex. Leslie felt this way about her father; therefore, Doris felt this way about Sam. This was very confusing to Doris, who again felt that her mother saw her as the bad little girl she apparently was.

The situation with Mac was a little different. Rather than attempt to sever the relationship between mother and son, Sam would inform Leslie that the boy needed to "man-up," that he needed to be subjected to some discipline. When Leslie would become defensive, he'd simply make certain that the next instance that Mac would come within range he would lash out at the child in front of his mother. When she would not move to protect the boy, her fear of him would become apparent to all.

Looking back, Doris can see the gradual dimming of her mother's ability to function even when she was functioning. More and more worn down by the constant criticism of herself and *her children*, Leslie seemed to only come home from work, fall asleep on the couch, wake up and then go to work again. The passive-aggressive mother now became the zombie mother—more dead than alive. Leslie remained this way for most of her early childhood.

As Leslie was sinking, Doris was being called upon to take up the slack within the household. Cooking, cleaning, looking after her brother—anything that she was capable of doing, that did not draw outside the family's attention to the fact that the family was not "normal."

Thus, grocery shopping was done by the parents but dishes fell to both the children. Clothes would be bought by the mother but the kids would be doing the laundry. The dishes would pile up, Sam would haul both kids out of their beds to do the chores and then he would belittle Leslie, often in front of her children.

Guilt was served in heaping portions and all three members were used to elicit it. As the mother felt guilty for working a full-time job and not managing the upkeep of a spotless home, the children were made to feel guilt that they had not helped their mother enough. Worse, the kids felt anger at their mother for not being stronger, or they felt anger toward the other sibling for not seeming to pull their fair share of the load dumped on them. None of them were allowed to voice any discomfort. The only vocalized complaints were issued by the head of the household.

One example of a method used to separate brother and sister is what Doris remembers as: The Washcloth Incident. A washcloth has fallen to the tiled floor of the bathroom. Mac and Doris are ordered into the bathroom and Sam proceeds to demand which of them dropped the washcloth and left it there. They are told that this endangers the household—someone could slip, fall and he does not have the time to take anyone to the hospital because one of them has been careless. They are informed that since their mother is not there to handle this situation he will have to. He demands to know who has been so careless.

Doris and Mac look at each other. Neither signal to the other any knowledge of the washcloth being on the floor. Sam whips off his military belt and proceeds to strike them in turn. No one owns up to the washcloth being on the floor. He strikes them again. Doris and Mac look at each other again, imploring the other to confess. No confession and the belt strikes again. He never leaves a mark that can be seen. Never.

Acts such as these served to separate Doris and Mac. In the beginning, it was Doris who would step in to protect her little brother from their mother. Doris could no longer protect Mac. The realization of this change in the dynamics hit both siblings hard. Both turned to a mother who was not there. Each, separately isolated. Each, separately believing what they were told to believe: They were worthless.

Perhaps due to their age difference, perhaps due to their personality or gender difference, the two siblings would interact with their agony differently. Doris would attempt to become wallpaper, the perfect student, and above all, make no waves. Mac would wet the bed and sometimes set fire to things. Their recollections of their mother would differ as well. Mac would say that: "Mother taught us how to survive." Doris would not agree: "No, Little Brother. She taught us how to be victims."

Chapter 5
Montana Bound

Sam returns from his isolated tour in Alaska. Coming back to Texas, the Airman is briefly home when he is transferred to Glasgow A.F.B. in Montana. Homelife is always thrown into turmoil when he returns.

Doris is not the same as when he left. Like everyone else around her, he does not notice that she does not fight to keep her puppy. None noticed that the light is dimmed, that even leaving Amigo produces little in the way of emotion. Why would they? Why should they? Her grades are perfect. Her manners are perfect. There is nothing to notice as she shuts the door of the last place to move to the new place.

In the years to come, Doris will hear the phrase: "Don't ask. Don't tell."[3] The phrase was created to explain a policy meant to protect those whose sexuality was not what the military culture felt comfortable with. Doris understands the underlying political current of that phrase. She understands this about her culture, her world, before the age of 10. They have a problem with it, so you can't talk about it. And we all know that opening your mouth has repercussions.

---

[3] https://en.wikipedia.org/wiki/Don%27t_ask,_don%27t_tell

The border between Canada and the United States is not far from the base housing they have been assigned to. This will be the fourth of eight grade schools she will attend.

After a conversation with someone at the base hospital she worked at, Leslie decides that Doris needs ballet, tap, and some tumbling. Aside from assuring that her body retains a flexibility that serves her to this day, there was little joy gained from these lessons. Lessons, that she already knew would stop once she began to develop a relationship with her teacher, once she began to find joy in the physical activity. And sure enough, the lessons stopped. Outside of school, the only constant activity was bowling.

Bowling was his game. He taught her. He signed her up in the leagues and took her to the weekly games. He was the coach. He was always present. She would be in bowling leagues for the entirety of her minority. She excelled at bowling, often having the highest average in the leagues she was a part of. Winning always feels good, even when the jailer is present.

Never having a father, how do you know how a father behaves? You know you feel uncomfortable with what is happening. Part of you is picking up that he is not comfortable with what he is doing. Non-verbal body language leaves clues of shame—shifting of eyes, an alertness to noise. He is watchful and seems careful of when and where these encounters occur. Then there is the secrecy he demands.

Texas shaped what Doris learned was normal in family life. She assumed her family was all "family." If she was uncomfortable with his unwanted attention, this was somehow because she was special in a way that held no benefits for her. If she hated what was happening, the adult taught her that this was her problem. She was to blame.

As she grew into adolescence, she learned that this was not so. Her beliefs unconsciously shifted to only Father-not-Fathers harming their daughters so. She would later have to sorrowfully, very sorrowfully face that genetic blood ties were not a barrier and neither was being a male. Doris-of-the-Future will face the reality of a daughter abused by her paternal grandfather, after assuring herself that the child would be safe from her demon. She would also learn of her brother's abuse. The sorrow is immense, as is the betrayal.

The fact of betrayal becomes a given in the world of Doris. This is how the world operates. The black and white television figures do not display her experience of the world. What is shown is not what is known. Therefore, the conclusion is that it is her lot, apparently, she is deserving of the treatment she receives, and no one else is made to suffer so. When puberty strikes Father-not-Fathers' game changes.

Now, he is telling her that the reason he does not penetrate her is because he does not want to cause a pregnancy. Now he is telling her that he is training her to be a good wife. Doris will learn later that he is sterile.

Mother always said that it was God's will that she never had a third child.

Chapter 6
The Fragility of Memory

For Doris, the apparent fragility of her memory has given her one more disparity to beat herself up with.

How is it that she has scars around her right eye but she has no memory of what happened? What she is told is a glass plate fell and she was in the wrong place at the wrong time. Why can't she remember that incident? The scar, the physical evidence of the reality of the event, runs from the outer mid-eye area down to the very top of her cheekbone. Shouldn't she carry some memory of the event? Facial wounds bleed severely and are quite frightening, there would have been lots and lots of blood!

Leslie reported that Doris fell out of a tree and that there had been some bleeding. Doris first heard this as a statement that her mother made regarding an accusation that was spat out about her not being a virgin by Sam, as he is later confronted for his actions. Was the bleeding between her legs? Was her mother saying that Doris had lost her hymen by falling out of a tree?

This is when Doris remembers the man saying that Sam had told him all about her. She does not relay this memory. She remains silent. Apparently, there was evidence seen by others, the adults, and the adults determined that yeah, sure, she is bleeding like this because she's fallen out of a tree?

The memory-not-memory is frustrating. Doris is grateful the memory does not carry with it flashbacks. More disconcerting is the growing evidence of those around her, those there to protect her don't seem to care.

Doris has very few memories prior to sixth grade. What memories there are appear to be primarily gleaned from what others have relayed. Most of what has been relayed has been by Leslie.

Imagine what Doris would give to know that as far as human memory is concerned, there is "...almost nothing before 3, little before 6." Neuroscientist Lisa Genova in 2021 states that "The thick fog of childhood amnesia lifts about the age of 6 or 7." "The development of language in our brains corresponds with our ability to consolidate, store, and retrieve episodic memories."[4]

The reason is language development. It turns out that you cannot personally, *directly* remember what you can't put into words. Said differently, in order for a memory to form, language must be present for the internal neurological process to be completed. It turns out that this is also why trauma blocks the formation, and the integration of memories.

According to what is known today: "All trauma is preverbal." Additionally, "Trauma by nature drives us to the edge of comprehension, cutting us off from language based on common experience or an imaginable past."[5] This new knowledge, one of the results of the studies of Vietnam veterans created a new entry for the DSM (Diagnostic and Statistical Manual). The new discovery was coined as Post Traumatic Stress Disorder—PTSD.[6]

---

[4] Genova, Lisa. Remember: The Science of Memory and the Art of Forgetting. New York: Penguin Random House LLC, 2021. pp. 86-87.
[5] Bessell Van Der Kolk, M.D., The Body Keeps the Score—Brain, Mind, and Body in the Healing of Trauma. New York: Penguin Books, 2014. Page 43.
[6] https://www.ptsd.va.gov/professional/treat/essentials/dsm5_ptsd.asp

Doris does not experience flashbacks. In her case, she strongly suspects she blacked out. Her body could not handle the stress placed upon it and she lost consciousness. The rest is just a guess, but when she blacked out the cover story became "falling out of a tree." Doris could not state the truth but as the title of Dr. Bessel Van Der Kolk's book proclaims: "The Body Keeps the Score." The story is accepted by the adults and their story stuck seemingly until Doris' mother, the nurse, proclaims what she might have suspected to be the truth all those years ago. Doris had been assaulted.

I'd like to take this opportunity to thank Doris. While it was necessary for the body to shut down, the body did not permanently shut down. While it was possible for our mind to replicate itself into separate personalities, the personality that was already in place was strong and flexible enough to withstand the complexity of this and other incidents.

Perhaps it would have been different if Doris had been a year or two younger. Perhaps it is genetic. Perhaps it is because of the strength of the bond with Grandmother Lynnette, which was formed so completely in the early years of life. It may even be plausible that in the early attempts to protect Brother, the fortitude to stand our ground garnered just enough strength to keep us from falling off the cliff of despair. Finally, there is yet another hidden strength learned and leaned on early in life.

It is in how strongly connected to "the tree" we reportedly fell from. Doris has never, nor will she ever, fall out of the majestic trees. The branches hold her. The leaves produce lullabies that move her ever closer to the wonder of the comforting skies, as it provides her glimpses further than she can see when grounded yet…. The roots, the strength of the trunk, all serve to keep her attached to that same ground. Solid, dependable, always waiting for her, the trees are a constant, consistent companion.

The trees are everywhere, no matter where she moves to. No matter where she is there is always the "meet and greet" of their familiarity. Nature saves. Nature nourishes. The trees ground her; they lend her their solid flexibility enhancing her spirit with the strength necessary to maintain her inner freedom. And when the God she prays to remains silent, her trees hold her in place. Even as the leaves drop, they never once forsake her. Spring always resurrects the greenery and sometimes there's the hidden wealth of flowers, birds, nuts and fruits!

As Doris gains in age there is also another constant she knows. The trees are everywhere she goes, and so are the schools and their libraries. Autobiographies, historical novels are consumed with regularity. Always a book. Always a new adventure, a new understanding, a new view of the world.

Yet, the books she would most have needed to read, the books that would have thrown so much-needed light onto her difficulties, did not exist in the public or school libraries of the late '50s or '60s. The 21st century knowledge is still beyond her searching and the Feminist Movement is just now beginning to rebirth itself. The day will come when "Our Bodies, Ourselves" is on the shelves.[7]

"But most of life's episodic memories are likely to be clustered between the ages of fifteen and thirty."[8] And so, let us proceed to

---

[7] The Boston Women's Health Book Collective, Our Bodies, Ourselves—A Book By and For Women. New York: A Touchstone Book Published by Simon and Schuster, 1973.

[8] Genova, Lisa. Remember: The Science of Memory and the Art of Forgetting. New York: Penguin Random House LLC, 2021. Page 87.

the 1960's. Let's proceed to a Doris who begins to paint with her own remembrances.

All Trees Are Oak Trees

Amid its branches the fairy dwell,
After soft rains and the suns' return.
Birds interweave their songs to sing,
As the little one is heard.

Small, strong hands grasp well-known paths,
As higher and higher she goes,
To the one lone place that's known to wait,
Alone now on her sacred throne.

Branches of bark, leaf and lark,
Sunlight filters through the eyes of elves,
This one has seen all of these, in this palace
All things dwell.

Reaching out she finds a leaf, a fan it now becomes.
An acorn fallen, beneath the tree—
Gold to be gathered,
Wealth that is won.

The realm is peaceful, all is right.
Triumphant, she envisions it all.
Her kingdom is safe for all who dwell.
To a young mind, nothing is small.

Chapter 7
An Offering of Solace

If there was some way to travel back in time, a way to present myself to Doris that would comfort and aid her, how would this best be accomplished? This is complicated.

The first thoughts are to sound major alarms, to scream, to wave your arms, then cry and sob and look to the stars in despair. Well, that's not going to help her! You already know that there is little she can realistically do to remove those harming her. She believes herself worthy of all the grief being sent her way. She is such a bad girl, of course, this is how she is to be treated. Even if these beliefs were not held, there is little within her power she can change.

Presenting her with the knowledge of the 21st Century regarding the new findings on childhood trauma, and sexual abuse is not likely to be comforting to a child still in grade school. Telling her she is not alone is not going to go far in aiding her in the midst of her solitude, her aloneness. History past and the history to come will grant her not one second of relief.

To know is not the same as benefitting from the knowledge. There are no counselors in the school systems that are likely to listen, no crisis lines to call, few believe children now, and in the 1960's she will be punished for her truth-telling. In that arena, not much has changed.

The more vulnerable you are, the more likely you are to be victimized, and the least likely you are to be heard. From what I know now and from what I knew from then, a child, any child, has to be very, very careful about who to trust.

How do you explain to a child, any child, the nature of this world they know all too well, and all too little of?

Let's begin with what you know has comforted you. Let's enhance her strength, her innate ability to see The Universe as safe. That ability is there, I know it is, and it is to this part of her we shall speak now.

And, so we begin....

Beneath the largest, oldest, most gnarly tree of a forest, I would set up a simple supper of homemade chicken noodle soup, freshly baked bread dripping with butter and honey, and a very delicate, but enormous, posy-painted, porcelain pot of jasmine tea. No sweetener is needed.

The scent of the tea would make her sigh and smile, as the slight bitterness would cut through the richness of the butter and the abundant, wild herbal sweetness of the honey. The soup, the soup has so very many memories attached to it. It will warm her in so very many ways.

If I could find a small stream within hearing and viewing distance, I would be so very happy to offer this to her too. Can there be the presence of wildflowers and, there must be birds!

I would spread, upon the ground, two quilts for us to lay ourselves comfortably upon. Both quilts are white, and for this one time, we are going to pretend that it is impossible for the lush grass to stain their purity. One quilt is made of embroidered blocks of a pastel floral wedding ring pattern, and the other is appliqued with a bright calico iris. Both, I will tell her, are made by the grandmothers.

As we partake of our banquet of bounty, I would tell her how I came to know how to make such a marvelously soothing, nourishing soup. "Grandmother Lynnette," I would tell her!

"Did you know, Doris, that Grandmother told me she always made the noodles fat because that was the way her grandchildren liked them?" I would then tell her of how Grandmother had whispered to me that she preferred her noodles the thinnest of thin.

"I made the noodles thin for her, did you know that?"

She will sigh as she tells me: "I wish I could do that."

I would then whisper prayerfully to her and to that wondrously Safe Universe that surrounds her: "You will!"

Chapter 8
The Second Tour Of Texas

After Glasgow, there was the usual change. Once again Sam was given an isolated tour. This time Sam decided that the remaining unit of three needed to be living in Salina, Kansas. Salina was Sam's hometown. His mother and his brother lived there and for the next year, the unit of three would be living there too. As per usual, as she is yet to reach her teens, there is little Doris remembers of this time period.

Oddly, none of the few existing memories have anything to do with Sam's people. There appears to have been little to no contact between his family and the unit of three. The "Grandmother" is Mrs. Miller, so it appears that she remarried. There is no grandfather around. There are no memories of picnics or any family gatherings. Nothing but nothing.

Of the memories that Doris does have, one is that behind the new abode there is a foot-wide space between the back fence and the thick shrubs. It's an area that she feels safe in. So safe that she sets up a kind of altar there.

Then there are carbonated lime sodas and the warm cashews she got from a pharmacy close by, and Mac attempting to do a trial run on some pilgrim candles he said he got for mother as Thanksgiving was soon.

The mattress that he subsequently caught on fire almost tore through the duplex they were living in and likely would have had it not been for Leslie's I-am-a-fireman's-daughter instincts kicking in and dousing the flames before more than the bedding burned. (The smell would be around for some time to come.)

Back from his Thailand assignment, everyone headed to Wichita Falls. This is a part of Texas, where dust devils roam and the sky reddens with clay when the winds pick up. Another change of space, another new set of teachers.

Shortly after the unit arrives, President Kennedy is assassinated in Dallas.[9] Doris remembers very little about the 22nd of November, 1963. The adults were very agitated and her new teachers, visibly upset.

Sam and Leslie must have been having some harder-than-normal financial difficulties when they first landed in the area because they would move to a very run-down flat next to a railroad. Leslie, of course, would land a nursing job at the hospital. Normally employers would be concerned by the job hopping, but as a military wife, it was understood that she followed her husband. Also, she was a veteran of the Korean Conflict, wasn't she?

Shortly after Leslie gained a new paycheck, they would move into a better location. It would result in both Doris and Mac needing to change grade schools in the middle of the school year. And again, shortly after that, the foursome would move to the small township of Burkburnett, closer to the base, and into a single dwelling house.

Yet again, the siblings changed schools. Doris remembers using the same English book. During this time period, she was diagramming sentences. Each move would find her either ahead or behind where her English class had been.

---

[9] https://en.wikipedia.org/wiki/Assassination_of_John_F._Kennedy

Finally settled into their new home and a new school system, a tornado hits the city they just moved out of.

What came to be known as "The Black Friday Tornado," hit Texas at 2:35 p.m. on the 3rd of April, 1964.[10] The path the F5 tore through the Wichita Falls area began in the northwestern section of the city. By the end of its trail, it would tear into and just past Sheppard Air Force Base, before finally exhausting itself and rising back up.

The weather observation tower by the flight line was not hit directly, but being one of the tallest buildings on base was definitely not a positive. The airmen, still contained within, reported that the building swayed. The small group decided to stay put because there had not been enough time for them to descend to the runway. It was told afterward, that there had been a lot of praying going on as they watched what would turn out to be over $10M worth of damage being wrought.

Another $5M would be the bill that Wichita Falls would be handed by the disaster. There would also be seven deaths. Those in the tower would not be among the casualties. Unfortunately, that would include Charles Sampson.

---

[10] 50 Years Later, A Look Back at 1964 Twister
Remembering the F5 Wichita Falls Tornado of April 3, 1964

Chapter 9

The Teacher Vs. The Nurse

At around fourteen years of age, something physical presented itself so public-facing that Leslie decided to take Doris to a doctor. It wasn't the beginning of her menses, although they were indirectly responsible—hormones being what they are.

It all began with a Physical Education teacher who had a teaching certificate the ink had barely dried upon. It was her freshman year, 9th grade, and in those days Texas P.E. teachers also taught Health. Doris heard from her new teacher that showering was better than bathing because you weren't laying in the water you were cleaning your body with.

Nurse Leslie got her undies all in a bunch regarding this statement being uttered. Most likely this reaction was because there was only a bathtub in the apartment they were living in at the time. The nerve ending that had been landed on was due to Sam being shipped off to Germany so, the remaining three members were removed from the house they had been living in. Even though Sam would be in a military barracks while still receiving the military allowance for a family, the threesome had once again been downgraded since he wasn't there.

Making an appointment to see this Know-It-All teacher became something of a mission for Nurse Sampson. In the course of the discussion, acne came up as a concern. The teacher queried the nurse if Doris was under the care of a dermatologist. Being a nurse, the teacher relayed that she was certain that Mrs. Sampson was aware that such severe acne could easily lead to lifelong scaring. So, off to the dermatologist Doris went.

Both adults would have been appalled had they known that Doris had attempted to take matters into her own hands, at one point using Comet on her face as a scrub to curb the raging eruptions. Needless to say, that only exacerbated the outbreak. Luckily Doris did not attempt to cure herself more than a couple of times in this manner.

It's estimated in today's world that approximately 85% of teens will present with acne. As our bodies shift into adolescence there are often imbalances as our hormones shift into reproductive mode. This is true for both sexes. Stress also comes into play as a factor in how critical acne may become. Doris was erupting, it's come to the attention of a teacher, and that is how Doris found herself under the care of a physician.

The nurse was there for the entire appointment, so even if Doris had thought to speak of the happenings at home, she would not have spoken with Mother there. Doris was still feeling the tension from The Teacher vs. The Nurse. Doris would not want the tensions that would have resulted from The Nurse vs. The Doctor.

But then again, the year is 1965, The Doctor is a dermatologist and the questions she would have been asked would not even remotely have delved into her situation.

Chapter 10
The Slusher Crush

Acne wasn't the only side effect of the onset of puberty. Looking back Doris can see that the first crush of her life shortly predated the acne. Doris was doomed the second she was assigned her first locker, her first seating in her first class. When she was first implanted into the Burkburnett school system, the alphabet, being what it is, the word "Sampson," will be just before the word "Slusher."

From her first day in school until the very day she would leave for Germany and her new high school in Kaiserslautern, just to the side of her, just to the front or back of her, would be Stevie Slusher. His locker was either to the left of her or to the right of her every single, solitary year. He was either sitting on the chair ahead of her or in the chair behind her in every class save gym.

It's said that each of us has unconscious likes and dislikes, attractions or let's say disinterest when it comes to our hormonally charged preferences. Doris would not be terribly surprised if those preferences would turn out to be: male, thin, blonde hair, nice smile. These descriptives, as it will turn out, will also be applicable to most attractions going forward.

He was a pleasant person. Always polite, always kind in action and words. He was also totally indifferent when it came to Doris. She would see him and he would smile the wonderful smile that he smiled for all other sentient beings. Nice guy. Just simply a really nice person. And for years Doris would become tongue-tied and plagued with periodic blushing each time he would say even a mere "Hi." This stalemate lasted for a couple of years. Then, their freshman year "Sadie Hawkins Day" changed the "Hi" to an uncomfortable silence.

For those who are not aware of the comic strip "Li'l Abner," the popularity of the long-running newspaper content actually made it to the wide screen in 1959 as a musical comedy.[11] The creator of the comic phenomenon was Al Capp. He dreamed up a hillbilly town called "Dogpatch." One of the major, ongoing themes of the strip is "Sadie Hawkins Day."

The mayor of Dogpatch had a daughter who was a spinster and he wanted to be rid of her. How to do this was a problem he pondered mightily. Then he finally found a way, and the solution was nothing short of inspirational! He proclaimed a new event, where the unmarried females of the town would be given the opportunity to marry one of the bachelors. All the bachelorettes had to do was...catch them.

At the starting line, on Sadie Hawkins Day, the single males would line up and when the shot was fired, they'd run for the hills. Shortly after, the second shot would send the single females off and running. This race would actually become part of the American culture. At the Burkburnett High School, the bachelorettes not only had to catch, but you had to feed the lucky guy!

Doris prepared a feast. Butter fried chicken and biscuits...Stevie was not going to starve.

On the day of the race, everyone is lined up and the running begins. Doris is one determined young girl. She chases that poor boy

---

[11] Li'l Abner (1959) - IMDb
https://en.wikipedia.org/wiki/Li%271_Abner

up one side of the campus and down the other. Doris cannot remember the actual length of time but bear in mind that Doris was capable of running a mile in those days. Luckily or unluckily, it appears that Mr. Slusher could too. He finally escaped by bursting into the boy's bathroom. As determined as she was....

That was some seriously fine chicken he missed out on, by the way.

Meanwhile, back at the lockers, an uneasy silence held until the day she left for Germany. That last day, in the middle of her sophomore year, he said that he'd heard she was leaving and that it was too bad because he was about to ask her out.

<SIGH>

Note to the reader: Be advised that these events have run through my mind, they have been re-remembered countless times. With each remembrance, I am certain the story...enlarged? (Stevie, if you are still out there, you've been one lovely memory. Thank you!)

Chapter 11
The Salvation And The Descent

"Christian baptism is the immersion of a believer in water in the name of the Father, the Son, and the Holy Spirit. It is an act of obedience symbolizing the believer's faith in a crucified, buried, and risen Savior, the believer's death to sin, the burial of the old life, and the resurrection to walk in newness of life in Christ Jesus."[12]

Doris remembers a yellowing, white leather-covered bible, that she had to zip open to gain access. At the end of the gold zipper was a cross. The pages within were thin and somewhat wrinkled because they had been left outside. She knows it belongs to her. She does not know how she came by it, or how it was lost, or how it had been left out in the dampness.

Doris is careful with books. She finds it very difficult to use a hi-lighter, or to mark or fold the corner of a page to remind her of where she was reading before laying a book down—there is a reason for bookmarks after all! In later years she will read not only the St. James Bible but many other religious texts. Books are sacred and are to be treated with respect. That this bible was damaged, in any way, is unusual. That it is missing is unusual.

She's fairly certain she no longer had it in her possession after grade school. During the time she spent in Salina, she had a private place along the back fence line, it is possible that it would have been

---

[12] https://www.baptistpress.com/resource-library/sbc-life-articles/understanding-baptism/

part of that space, but she does not recall it being there. Montana holds no memory of this possession. To the best of her recollection, it existed only during the first time she had lived in Texas. For certain, the weathered bible was no longer with her when the family again landed in Texas.

After being stationed at Sheppard AFB for several years, Sam would be shipped off to Ramstein AFB in Germany. He would reside there for about two years before the remainder of the family unit would cross the ocean to join him. It won't be until the middle of her sophomore year of high school that Doris, Leslie, and Mac will travel to Germany, residing there until the winter of 1969. During this lovely, left-alone time period, Leslie found religion.

Religion was among many topics that Doris does not remember ever having been part of the limited family conversation. Part of the cloak of silence within the household was likely due to at least one of the parents often sleeping after their varied work shifts. Part of it was also likely because it was easy, too easy to get on the wrong side of Sam's moods. Leslie, with Sam around, was mostly numb.

Doris had been baptized at birth, as is the Methodist tradition. Perhaps this is when the bible is gifted to her. Leslie, Doris assumes, was a Methodist. It is an assumption because this will be the first time that Doris is aware of her mother's religious side.

Doris does not know, but strongly suspects, that Leslie was never married in a church. Perhaps there was a chapel of some kind when she married James, but that ceremony was likely done somewhat secretively as the Navy was not notified that either the Ensign or the Chief Petty Officer had married. The marriage ceremony with Charles carries no memory but there again, Leslie is not wanting to draw the attention of her mother. Lynnette with knowledge of a pending marriage to Charles would not have been easily navigated.

Until this time period, Doris does not remember any member of the unit stepping foot in a church. Yet, now the threesome is attending regularly. For the first time, Doris is in a community situation, on a regular basis, outside of the public school systems. The threesome became regulars, attending service, outside events, and, of course, there was Sunday School.

Every Sunday, from the pulpit, the call goes forth for those who would join the congregation. Full immersion baptism in front of this Southern Baptist congregation promised full forgiveness of the past. The sin-filled would be cleansed and freed, to be reborn, anew into this world, this community of believers. It wouldn't take long, it wouldn't take a lot of thought, all it took was what she had been told over and over and over—she was bad, she was not worthy.

Within this community, she is presented with the promise of salvation from all her past discrepancies. Her early teen years are filled with hormones, acne, and a lot of internalized misery. She is just beginning to see that this family unit of hers is not all that has been presented to her. By now she is seeing her mother away from Sam, a mother who is more alive than dead. It is the religion that is reviving Leslie. Doris reaches for this newly found elixir of life.

Apparently the first baptism didn't take, so Doris took the second dive, this time Southern Baptist. The experience was freeing. The weight of her internal struggles modified to a point of almost seeming to never have existed. It is hard to describe the buoyancy of spirit she attained after this immersion. Doris will come to understand that there is another word for this phenomenon: catharsis. She will learn that there are many paths that will aid in freeing her spirit, but for now, how this process works is solely connected to her baptism.

The first half of her sophomore year of high school would be remarkable, spring-like. The acne would diminish, "Stevie" would smile at her again, and all too soon she would board the plane to fly over the Atlantic. Within the first 24 hours, her spirit would again be caged.

Chapter 12

That Second Half of Her Sophomore Year

If you display a dislike for something, it will be used to punish you. If you like something, it will be used to punish you. If you show no response—most of the time, invisibility works. It's a total no-win. It wasn't what Doris felt, or needed, wanted, or did, that brought down the inquisition. The reality is that powerless people need to feel powerful, and they will feed voraciously on anything within their grasp. This is something to burn into your brain in the event you seek salvation. What Doris is learning as she steps onto German soil is that: If the door to hell is not removed from your life, the devil returns.

Germany in January is generally grey, and rather like wrapping yourself in a damp, heavy wool cover that somehow doesn't heat you but chills you. As Doris remembers this scene, it is descriptive of not only the world outside her skin but also, her internalized picture of what awaits her inner world as she steps off that plane. There is Sam. It is not a joy-filled reunion.

The newly united foursome settles into the car for the drive to Ramstein Air Force Base. The family will be spending the night on base and then move into their rented, 2nd floor, 3-bedroom apartment the following day. After the group has somewhat settled in, Sam says that he and Doris are going to go to the apartment to check to see that all is ready in preparation for the move.

It takes about a half hour to get to Weilerbach. They return in time for dinner that evening, almost 3 hours later. Leslie comments on how tired Doris is looking, how the trip across the Atlantic seems to have truly worn her out. Her eyes are bloodshot, swollen. She must be very, very tired.

As per usual, everything is fine. No questions as to why it took three hours. The husband and wife have been apart for two years and yet, nothing is questioned as to why Doris was the family member Sam requires to check on the new abode. Leslie is apparently noticing Doris but the concern is that she needs sleep, big day on the morrow—the apartment needs the kitchen stocked and their personal items will be arriving by noon.

Finally settled into the new jailhouse, it's time to get acquainted with the new school system. To get to school both siblings need to board the school bus which stops about a 15-minute walk near the town's center. The apartment they have moved to is located close to the outer rim of the growing town. It's new enough that the road outside is grated but not yet paved. They walk together and in the dark. For most of the remaining school year, they will arrive at the bus stop in the dark and return to the bus stop at near dusk.

If you've never been off of American soil, you don't quite get just how young our country seems to European eyes. Landing in Germany was an eye-opener. For instance, the town was founded in the 1760s but it had been in existence for a few hundred years prior.

In the 1960s much of Weilerbach's downtown is still cobblestone roads. The cobblestone road butts up against a concrete curb, immediately followed by the concrete sidewalk that sits right next to either steps that lead to a door, or the doorway itself. Visually, it reminded Doris of all the black-and-white movies she had seen with vampires being the main characters. Add in the darkness when they would arrive at the bus stop in the morning, and the darkness that awaited when they descended from their trip back, Doris developed a penchant for crosses.

Warding off the vampires? Mentally, perhaps it was easier to have an intense wariness of the receded doorways and the older-than-old churches with their adjacent cemeteries than to worry about the return to the known threat that awaits. As Doris is collecting crosses, she is also covering the bathroom door with a washcloth—a defensive move to prevent an all too real keyhole-pepping-Sam from invading even this privacy.

After the 30-minute bus ride, there is the predominately concrete, former military billeting, dull grey and even duller green building that the Army has designated for the high school. After the Texas sun and the fairly new high school campus she came from, this does nothing to encourage her spirit.

Kaiserslautern American High School has a library, of course, but again nothing like the ones she had access to. The public libraries will be, of course, German public libraries. And, even though she knows that this cannot be a true vision of what she sees, all she sees are pine trees. Pine trees are one of the few trees that do not invite her to climb. Her world appears to be colored in only various shades of fatigue green and brown on a background of grey.

Then, there are the new classmates. Even though she has gone to many, many new schools, those schools were in the middle of the country that she's no longer residing in. New to her is the diversity, and she is not quite certain how to interact with the students. The last few years of schooling in Texas had her cautiously peering out of her shell. Now, this additional newness finds her retreating again, as she tries to find her bearings in this new, old world.

Most of the schools she attended in The States were primarily white. Now she is looking at a sea of colors, and the accents are as varied. And, it's not only the students but the teachers and school staff as well. By the time Doris graduates high school, she will have had an English teacher who is English. She will have a Geometry teacher who is Norwegian. Although she does not take a "foreign" language class, here a Frenchman teaches French and a German is teaching German. All this has the effect of shutting her down. She becomes more wallpaper-like than ever. Paler than ever. Muted. For the first time in her life, her grades begin to fall. Since no one really notices, no one really notices, no one really notices....

Perhaps if the changes had not been so varied, perhaps if the alterations had not been so one after the other, perhaps if the entire culture and language and scenery had not been so unknown, perhaps then she might have garnered enough spirit to seek assistance.

Doris is living in an apartment in the middle of a foreign country, and nothing takes on even the remote appearance of a life-saver. The religious community she had been attached to has disappeared and it appears that Leslie too, suddenly has no interest in religion.

She is adrift, numb, and for the moment just keeping up just enough appearance for appearance's sake. The last thing she needs is added complication, in the complexity she is already experiencing. Luckily, spring will come, her sophomore year will end, and the beginning of her junior year is but a few months away.

Chapter 13
The Return of Spring

When spring arrives and sophomore year is completed, a new world opens to Doris. The family has not changed one bit but the greyness is gone. Birds, trees, flowers from every window box greet her as she is finally free to walk around the town. She is a few months from her 16th birthday. The simple ability to walk around on her own is freeing.

The township is not threatening in the summer sunshine. The shops open their doors and the people are friendly… but not friendly. Doris can't tell if the barrier is her or them, or what is most likely, a combination of the two. Although Doris does not speak German, many Germans speak English. During the time she is there, she will notice that many of the older women primarily wear black— a lot of widows and a scarcity of older men. It will finally dawn on Doris that WWII ended in 1945 and what she is noticing is one of the results of that war.

She's pretty much able to roam free, but that doesn't amount to much as Doris does not drive. There were some lessons in Texas, through high school, but in Germany, the price of insurance for anyone under the age of 18 is so high that a vast majority of her classmates do not drive.

There is one planned activity. There is always one planned activity when Sam is present. He's signed her up, yet again, into a bowling league. The bowling alley is located on base, a half-hour drive from Weilerbach. The dependent's league is on Saturday. Of course, he drives her. Of course, he coaches her. Of course, he is always present. She continues accumulating the trophies that are placed atop the cabinet. Her Brother does not bowl, but it doesn't occur to Doris to question that. Sam continues to keep them separate. Separate bedrooms, separate activities, and always with him present. In Mac's case, it becomes the Boy Scouts.

When she is not going to school, she does not have access to books. There likely was a library on base but no one mentioned it and she didn't think to ask, and it was definitely beyond her walking distance. At this time, they do not have a television and even if they did everything would be German except for the Armed Forces Network.

The network also had at least one radio station but the music was primarily from the 40's and very early 50's. In the afternoons, around 4 p.m., there was one hour of current hits. The foursome would not receive a television until they moved into dependent housing not far from their high school in Kaiserslautern. That move would be over a year into the future.

The German food was amazing! Doris has always been something of a biscuits and gravy kind of gal. The schnitzels, the dumplings and kraut, the strudels, all found their way to her plate. She was feeling more comfortable with her surroundings now and beginning to acclimate. It had taken longer than normal but she was stabilizing.

The prison still exists, of course. New place, new people, same rules—his rules.

Chapter 14

Serendipity and the Life of Honorable Choice

ser·en·dip·i·ty

[ˌserənˈdipədē]

NOUN

1. the occurrence and development of events by chance in a happy or beneficial way:

    "a fortunate stroke of serendipity" · *"a series of small serendipities"*[13]

There are constants in the life of Doris. Winter becomes spring, which becomes summer, which becomes fall, which becomes winter again. The cycle of nature repeats no matter the who, the what, or the where. There's the sunlight on your face or moonlight bathing the night, and let's not fail to mention the stars winking back at all of us—these are constants. But as Doris learned at an early age, the other constant is change. The universe is full of paradoxes.

There is one potential change that she does not want above all others—she does not want to become what she hates. Might, the opportunity to overpower another, does not make it right. The

---

[13]https://www.bing.com/search?pglt=41&q=definition+of+serendipity&cvid=9b a25f6c7e3d4f1496aef6c4a2479bcb&aqs=edge.0.0l9.7068j0j1&FORM=ANSPA 1&PC=ASTS

potential, the ability to do harm does not mean that you should. There is a choice. You should not attempt to control others, but you can choose to control you. It's far too easy to engage in the hierarchy, the pecking order that she's been subjected to.

She may fear him, but she sees him. He has no friends. Sam lacks integrity. He is not honest with himself or with others. He is not strong. He is weak and, in that weakness, he strikes out at everything and everyone else that he perceives as somehow weaker. Doris does not want to become Sam. She does not see Leslie as a role model either.

Capitulating time and time again to fears instead of facing them is not a habit any adult should be getting into. We are not alone in our lives. We are part of a community of others who will be affected by this victimization, this abuse. A community of others who will be affected by our individual choices, just as we are affected by theirs.

The closer in proximity someone is to you, the higher the probability that someone is imitated. Said differently, we learn from who and what surrounds us. None of us are born speaking as we emerge from the womb. As we learn to talk and walk, we also learn the ins and outs of being a human being.

If you are abused, you are being taught how to abuse. If you are a victim, you know how to victimize. Do not reach for the forbidden fruit of their tree of knowledge. You already know what they are doing is wrong, now let it sink in that *they* know what they are doing is wrong.

Do not poison yourself. If you need further encouragement not to become your abuser, take a very clear-eyed look at that person. Do you really want to be them? Do you really want someone to feel like you do? Do you want anyone to feel this way about you? Do you want to feel this way about yourself?

If you are being abused at this time, you may not find a safe way to rid yourself of this plague, but you can choose not to infect another. The person afflicting you learned how to abuse you before they choose to abuse you. Break the chain. Do not be the next weakened, sickened link.

Do not become what you hate. It will destroy the integrity of your life as you can well see, even in this moment, how they continue to destroy their own lives and how they are taking down others with them.

Doris knows this is hard to do. She fights it daily, but she knows that if she does not maintain her integrity, the struggle back must be monumental because these people are not getting any happier, they are not thriving.

Being the best person you can be, under any set of circumstances, is to be applauded. I now applaud Doris. Hell, I'm making this a standing ovation! BRAVO, My Wild Thing! Because you've kept it together you are about to become the winner of a get-out-of-jail-free card. Serendipity happens, and if you've kept your integrity, you can reap what you have sowed.

Chapter 15

Her Junior Year

The cycle of Nature repeats and time waits for no one. Doris turns 16 with no fanfare. There hasn't been a genuine birthday party celebration since Grandmother Lynnette presented her with a wonderful angel food cake with silver sprinkles all over the over-the-top meringue-like white frosting—one of the few memories of childhood before the age of six. No matter, Doris is too busy dreading the return to school for the first time in her life.

It's getting darker sooner, as the days repeat the cycle of the seasons. Summer is quickly turning into fall. No longer is there time for the wonderful walks along the countryside. She returns to the weekday trudge back and forth to the bus stop.

It's more familiar now, and Doris has taken to not wearing one of her collection of crosses. She even has developed a fondness for the old churches and cemeteries—very old by American standards. Perhaps "trudge" is no longer the appropriate description. This walk back and forth to board the bus for the 45-minute trip to school is now something of an oasis.

She knows the folks who run the bakery that is across from the bus stop. Instead of focusing on the dreariness, she now inhales the wonderfully aromatic fresh bread that fills the air, remembering the friendliness of the shop keepers. It's better. It's more comfortable. At least, it's not home. At least, it's not school.

The school atmosphere is antiseptic, at best. Drab. Very drab. The other students and the teachers are all kind of a blur. The few smiles she elicits cannot be followed up with potential friendship, as there is no time between classes for this to happen. Every day is regulated by the school system or the home.

It irks her that her grades are not what they have been. Part of the difficulty is that in Texas the mathematics curriculum was Algebra I, Algebra II, Geometry, then Trigonometry. The Kaiserslautern system is Algebra I, Geometry, Algebra II, Trigonometry. Doris barely squeaked by in Algebra II, after changing to the new school. So, she thought, okay, we'll backtrack and do Geometry. Bad move.

She's not in the best of spaces to begin with. What's new, right? Let's throw in a Norwegian teacher, with a fairly heavy accent, and quite frankly at this stage she probably should have totally ditched mathematics. The problem wasn't the teacher. Not really. The problem is that Doris didn't really learn Algebra I or II.

The Texas system was taught in such a way that rote memory got you through the classes. Not so in this European-like school system. Said differently, one plus one does equal two but Doris does not understand why…not at the level required for the "higher" classes. Rote memory alone does not aid you when it comes to the higher classes.

Understand that when Doris is feeling like such a dope about her grades, the reality is that for the first time in her life, she did not receive all "A's." Yeah, no 4.0 last semester. If a parent had been concerned, or if a teacher had expressed concern, perhaps the discussion could have proved beneficial to her ego. This did not happen for many reasons. Some of these reasons are the already familiar ones, just a slightly different beat on a slightly different set of drums.

Like Ramstein A.F.B., the school is over a half-hour drive from Weilerbach. Doris does not drive. She has to catch the bus which leaves within minutes of her last class. No extra-curricular activities are possible without her parents' willingness to provide transportation.

If she speaks to a counselor…well, she does not know how to speak to a counselor as she's never had one speak to her. Her parents are disengaged when it comes to her future, which neither they nor she are speaking about. Her whole being feels like a disengaged, underwatered plant—she's alive but she's receiving no nourishment.

Folks talk about living in the present. That is all Doris does. Leslie has numbed down again and is back to her zombie routine of work-couch-work-couch. Religion appears to have been vanquished. The only other activity is the damn bowling. Thinking about the past is painful to the point that she never contemplates thinking about a future she apparently has no control over whatsoever. Perhaps she is taking after her mother after all….

The lull before the storm, the eye of the hurricane, Doris doesn't know this but she is on a precipice. Her stillness has a wariness, an edge to it. What's next? Is it possible to be numb enough not to contemplate suicide? Wallpaper never contemplates removing itself, does it?

The next few years are a whirlwind. Please forgive her if she missteps, or misremembers. It's very confusing to have your world turned upside down so very many times. What's coming is an act of so very many tosses and turns, it makes the past pale in comparison. Doris will suddenly become very conscious that her inner balance is threatened. And yet….

Chapter 16
The Airman

Being in Germany meant that this would be the first time that the family unit had been overseas together. Sam's isolated tours provided much-needed periods of peace for Leslie, Doris, and Mac. This isolated tour was not like the others. Sam did not return. They had followed him.

Military families on foreign shores have customs that are generally not as stringently followed stateside. While overseas, military families are expected to host the single, enlisted personnel during some holidays. Thanksgiving and Christmas, in particular, are seen to be of import. It is reasoned that since some have their families with them, these fortunate families should host the single members who are unable to make it stateside to be with their families. And so, for the first time Doris can remember, they are going to have company coming.

Doris does not know how the two airmen were selected. Sam had spent close to two years in the barracks at Ramstein, and those who were coming worked in the Weather Squadron, so he knew the guests that arrived. As to whether Sam had decided which two were coming, or if the custom was to draw names out of a hat, or some other form of selection, Doris does not know. She knows that one was doing the same job as Sam, a weather observer. The other airman was a technician with the squadron. The two coming shared a room together in the barracks. Both were in their very early 20's.

Leslie went all out. Sam was unusually enthusiastic about impressing the two men. The eggnog prepared was particularly potent having a pint each of dark rum and bourbon. It was way too smooth. It was quite the event and Sam, in particular, was very pleased with what Leslie had cooked up for his guests.

The men were of about the same height and on their best behavior. Glenn was the heavier of the two, with dark, almost black, thick hair. Both had great smiles but Gary, in contrast, was blond and slim. No one knew it then, and all would be very surprised to know it would be less than three years hence, that Glenn would be Gary's Best Man. Doris is meeting her husband for the first time.

Shortly after the holiday festivities, Doris would learn that Gary has asked Sam's permission to date her. Looking back, some say, gives a person twenty/twenty vision. When Doris looks back, it is more like a multi-dimensional, layered universe of if, and, but, or maybe.

It could be that Sam was sensing a loosening of the bondage he had forged. It could be that Sam felt that it was inevitable that Doris would begin to date, now that she is sixteen. If she began dating someone her age, she might begin to form relationships with that person's parents. Why not present her with a dating option that he knew and perhaps, felt he could control?

Doris reacts by going somewhat into shock over the fact that, apparently, someone is finding her attractive. She holds her breath and somehow, as bewildering as it seems to both her and Leslie, Sam gives his permission for her first date to be with someone five years her senior.

Every date she is taken out to dinner and they are dating close to four times a week, depending on his schedule. For someone who has led a life very much confined to either school or the home, this is like a fantasy come true. For crying out loud, she's even learning how to use chopsticks!

Like Sam, Gary is a rotating shift worker. As Doris is still in high school their outings are usually in the evening hours. There will be weeks where they are only able to meet twice in a given week, on his days off. Later, when school is out for the summer, they will go on day trips such as to Heidelberg or Nuremberg. A whole new world was opening up for Doris.

Their dating would begin just after that Thanksgiving dinner, and they would be lovers by Christmas. Lucky for Doris, he uses a condom. They are both infatuated. The attention she is receiving has totally engulfed her world. She is happy and it's showing in her demeanor. Sam continues to be the plague he is, and he is noticing a change in her that he does not like when he commands her to his bed.

There's a shift in her manner of being. He does not like it and suddenly, he's given the opening to appear parental while not appearing to dismiss the relationship he's approved of. Doris should never have been so concerned about her "B" in Algebra II, because now she has a "D" in Geometry. Sam grounds her. How could anyone possibly have a problem with his parental concern?

She'll still be allowed to see Gary, but only on the non-school days and if that happens to be when he's working, they'll just have to not see each other for those weeks. There's no parental concern expressed by either parent about why the low grade happened. No conversation with the teacher. No questions as to why the grade is what it is. Leslie is totally silent during all of this.

Sam's action does not have the result he wants. Doris is not cowering sufficiently. All this does is get her back up. She's angry, not complacent. It's a cold anger, and not one she's used to feeling.

It certainly isn't one he's used to interacting with. What he does not know is that Gary has proposed, she's accepted, and they're both waiting until she is eighteen and stateside.

Since neither parent bothered to contact the school regarding her grades, it was easy for Doris to drop Geometry and take a study hall. She was told no more "D's," well, that was not going to be a problem anymore. All Doris now needed to do was wait until the last report card of her junior year and she'd no longer be grounded.

It worked. However, Sam is now seeing that the relationship, the bond between the two are stronger than he expected. The summer between her junior and senior years, Sam is stewing and brewing up another way to tighten his control. This time he's out to break the relationship, and possibly even finding a method that will keep her bound to him for the rest of her life. He's going to use blackmail.

Chapter 17
The Destruction of a Christmas Tree

The Penalty of Knowledge

Do not pass through.
There is no passing through.
Once known, it will never be unknown.
Knowledge hurts and heals as it binds and protects.

What must be said is hard to hear.
What is hard to hear is remembered.
Darkened corners, once lit,
Become the cross we bear together, forever.

Doris did not know there was a name for what he did, not until Abu Ghraib—waterboarding.[14] Only, it wasn't water, it was gin.

Periodically, since grade school, Sam would keep Doris out of school on a day Leslie would be working. Mac would be in school and Leslie never questioned the absences, likely because she never knew of them. The school systems never questioned absences when each absence was accompanied by a written excuse from a parent.

---

[14] Waterboarding - Wikipedia
Ex-CIA Officer Who Destroyed Waterboarding Videos: Torturers "Disgusted" at Being Labeled "Torturers" | Common Dreams

It didn't happen often, but often enough that it wasn't suspicious. This was such a day.

This day was different.

He had tied her hands and feet and blindfolded her. Nothing even remotely like this had happened prior. She could not see what he was up to, so when he began by telling her to drink, she had no idea what she was being told to consume. For a decade now, Doris has been able to numb herself to what he did. Not this day. The fear that set on her was intense, and he had restrained her in anticipation of that fear. Fear that he had experienced, no doubt, during his military training.

When she would not drink, he would pinch close her nose, which would result in her gasping for breath and then swallowing some more of the foul stuff. She has no idea how much she consumed. When he determined there was enough in her, Sam untied her hands and feet and guided a still blindfolded, very clumsy, very dazed Doris into his bed.

Removing the blindfold, Sam got into the bed and, as was normal, covered them both with the sheet. Doris always closed her eyes during these episodes but she could tell that it was dark and that the curtains were likely closed.

Suddenly, the sheet was yanked off and there were flashes as the lights came on and the Polaroid black and white took a picture.[15] Sam gave out a sick laugh. The sound he emitted was not next to her on the bed, but coming from the source of the camera's flash.

---

[15] https://en.wikipedia.org/wiki/Polaroid_Swinger

Doris had never felt such a surge of adrenaline in her life. Wildly awake, she bounded out of the bed. Sam sneered, as he handed the still-developing shot to a naked Mac.

"What are you going to do," Sam asked, "when I show that picture to Gary?"

"He will kill you, you idiot!"

Immediately after she exploded with these words, Mac mumbled that the shot was over-exposed. Doris shot him a steely gaze and started heaving up her stomach contents, passing out.

There would never, ever be a conversation between them regarding these events. No conversation with Sam. No conversation with Mac. The situation is escalated now. Sam's fear level is heightened and this is the first time his fear is visible. It is very visible.

Will he believe that the siblings will remain silent? Perhaps he believes that they will attempt to protect each other. Perhaps he believes that neither wants Leslie to know. The status quo, the sameness, the not wanting to rock the boat silence has been the norm for a decade now.

In 1968, Doris is not seven but seventeen. What has happened has registered FULLY. What is known cannot be unknown and this sick, abusive game of his has now included a third person. The equation has changed dramatically. The violence has changed dramatically. As for Mac....

Had he approached her about what happened, had she approached him, would either of these potential conversations have changed a damn thing? Doris does not know. Doris will never know. Mac is dead and cannot be communicated with at the point of this writing.

What Doris does know is that there was never an apology. There was silence. There was life after this incident that went on as if nothing had happened to her, to him, to their relationship. Mac has been dead to Doris for a very long time. For a very long time, Doris will not be aware that this is exactly what she feels toward her brother—nothing. The betrayal is never forgotten nor forgiven. Never. How could it be, it was never discussed or alluded to? It was never buried, so the corpse just rotted away in full view....

Just forget about it. Nothing happened that you need to report. By inference, it is the same as saying that nothing has happened which was of import. It is the same as saying that what has happened to you holds no importance, but it is somehow important enough that you do not speak of it. What pains Doris most, as this is written, is that she knows so very many others know this pattern. So very many others have been deceived and devalued by this same deafening silence. So many others...including Mac.

Part of what reruns Doris' mindset is her visceral, full-throated verbal reaction to Sam's stated threat. Where did that vehemence come from? The surety in her voice and stance at that moment were such that both Sam and Mac were momentarily knocked back, unbalanced. I now refer to the letter that Leslie handwrote to Doris 25 years later:

"Of course, when you were 16 the shock came. You and Gary met me at the back of the ward as I got off at midnight and told me what had been going on since I first married Charles. I sent you to friends for the night. Gary made an appointment with the legal office and went with me. I was told that I could do nothing as it would be hearsay. You would have to bring the charges—I don't know why you wouldn't. The chaplain I talked with would only say we should forgive him. That was a big help. I wrote your grandmother to see if I could send you to her. You decided not to go."

Gary and Leslie dropped Doris off, returning to the apartment to confront Sam. The waterboarding episode has not been mentioned to Gary or Leslie. She has decided not to bring anything to do with her brother to their attention. That's for Mac to do.

Doris cannot say with certainty if she purposely determined to avoid that information because she sought to protect him one last time. However, if things were to go south, if things got out of hand, he hopefully would not be further damaged as well. Much of what Doris did at this time was "instinctual," for lack of a better word. What she did took guts. What she did was guttural.

Bringing Gary into the situation will result in keeping her out of Sam's bed, but not totally out of his reach. Even as the opportunity to come forward presented itself that night, Mac did not speak. Perhaps it was because as Sam was confronted, he became violent. He's been found out. He's been reported. Worse, those who have been reported to FULLY believe his victim. Additionally, he knows that there is more that could have been reported. He is trapped.

Sam lashes out. He couldn't hit Gary and he couldn't hit Leslie because of Gary. (Luckily there were no pets.) Unable to handle himself and not able to access his normal "outlets," Sam resorts to trashing the Christmas tree.

Chapter 18
Memories Clash

It is true that memory changes over time. Science tells us that each time we touch upon a memory, each time we remember, our minds alter the remembrance. Remember, as in reassembling. It's a process that aids us as a species in evolving within our world, but it does have its downside. It's not that Leslie purposely lies, it's that in her remembering she's altered a few things.

Doris and Gary also have the same, shall we say "alterations" going on in their minds. Five human beings will have five sets of memories stored that will change each time they are remembered. It cannot be stressed enough that the sooner a conflict is resolved, the better it will be for all involved. Time does not heal all wounds, it creates disparities in the record of events, and if you are a victim the ground beneath your feet is pretty shaky already.

It's not that Doris purposely has little compassion to offer Leslie. A 17-year-old Doris has as much sympathy to offer Leslie, as Leslie likely had to offer Lynnette at the same age. Even when a human reaches adulthood, all of us are only as good as what we have been taught, what we've done with what we're taught, and our level of understanding of what we truly don't understand. Ignorance is not bliss, it's bias. Ignorance is not bliss, it's handicapping.

Compassion requires knowledge. If the knowledge required is not present, compassion transforms into pity. Pity is a disservice to all involved with it, both sender and receiver. Pity is a form of hierarchy. From this "elevated" perch of morality, your integrity is damaged.

"Lying" is generally done out of fear and fear is not a place to attempt to gain any knowledge other than thou shalt not act out of fear. One of the problems with lying is that you end up lying to yourself, and that truly compounds the problem. It's really hard to go back and fix something that you don't now think of as being broken. In Leslie's case, how do you apologize or regret what you don't believe you were responsible for?

Since our memories do change it is very, very helpful to write it down. If you are experiencing abuse, this is something difficult to do. Discovery of your writing of events as close as possible to when they occur can bring repercussions. If you can find a safe place for your writings, do so.

If you are not being abused, journaling is a good habit to have if for no other reason than it will become a record of the past to which you can refer, refresh, revisit. Journaling will aid your "remembering."

One of the powers of the abuser is their ability to hide in the fog of the past. A past, that so often, so many would rather forget. So many will forget. I know I have forgotten some things that I now find in my journals or letters, and I'm guessing you will too. The longer the time period between the event and confrontation, the more difficult the process to heal and to mend relationships. Uppermost in your mind must be your safety in this pursuit. Please be safe.

Speaking of the difficult…. It is very difficult to perform triage when you are one of the wounded that lay on the battlefield. Doris has stretched herself about as far as she can go at this point. Leslie is somewhat shell-shocked, Sam is outed, so it falls to Gary. Leslie's written memory of what happened next does not match either Doris's or Gary's.

Leslie has written that she and Gary went to the legal affairs office and that they were told that nothing could be done unless Doris brought charges. Leslie goes on to state that this process stopped because Doris would not bring charges. The following quotation is taken from an email sent 32 years later, in the year 2000. This is from Gary in response to an inquiry into what he remembered of that time period:

"After you told me what was happening, I thought of going directly to the legal affairs people, but all I could've offered was heresy and third-party testimony. That left me with only the Chaplain as someone with whom to discuss the matter and try to find a course of action.

After that initial meeting, the three of us, you, Les, and I, had another meeting with the Chaplin and then, I think, Les had a follow-up with just the two of them. Anyway, from what you said, things changed shortly after that with no further/subsequent—shall we say—recurrences.

What, exactly, or even if anything, Les did, I don't know."

Doris has no memory of being asked to testify. From Gary's email, I think it is safe to say that Doris was never asked to testify to something that appears never to have been legally reported either by Gary or Leslie, much less Gary and Leslie together. The Chaplain appears to be Gary's action.

Gary reports that he initiated contact with the Chaplain then Doris, he, and Leslie met with him. There appears to be a meeting set up with Charles and Leslie attending. Doris remembers a meeting with the Chaplain and she only, during which he seemed mostly concerned that she has not become a prostitute. To borrow what Leslie wrote in her letter: "That was a lot of help."

The only other remembrance is of Sam, Leslie, and Doris's kneeling before the chapel altar and the Chaplain's prayers concerning forgiveness. Doris does not remember the presence of Mac. Doris does not remember an apology from anyone. Doris does not remember remorse from anyone other than Sam. Sam's remorse was solely that he had been caught.

If Leslie sent an inquiry to Grandmother Lynnette, the true reason for requesting that Doris live with her in San Jose was not mentioned. Grandmother would not be told of the abuse until shortly before Leslie wrote her letter to Doris in 1993—twenty-five years later. Doris does not believe that Leslie made the inquiry. That said, the sanctuary of her grandmother was offered.

Doris does remember turning down that offer. Not wanting to be separated from Gary and already in her last year of high school, such a move was not feasible for her. Doris would regret that. About a month later, she will find out that her world is changing yet again.

Sam is no longer a direct threat, but Gary has been assigned to California, just as the family unit is being moved into military family housing in Kaiserslautern. They will be separated by an ocean for a little over a year before they marry, in the meantime Gary is gone and Sam still remains.

Gary and Doris are told that wearing an engagement ring would be inappropriate, unseemly as she has yet to graduate from high school. Sam still remains and he's exerting his tattered authority within the unit again. The entire world does not know what the unit of now five members knows and the Chaplain is, after all, a Chaplain.

Once again, Doris is met with a wall of silence. The abuse she has been subjected to is so appalling that it cannot be mentioned either inside or outside the confines of the immediate family unit, but apparently not so appalling that her mother is not only remaining married to her rapist but still allowing him to sway over her. Doris considers this to be inappropriate and unseemly.

This is also the time period where Doris should have been asking some questions of her husband to be but she didn't. She can't get beyond the fact that he is leaving. She doesn't get beyond the point that in about a year she will be his wife. No thoughts get beyond the point that she is going to be living happily ever after as Mrs. Gary T. Riley. Her castle awaits, fully equipped with her white knight.

There are no white knights and it will fall to Doris to learn this the hard way. Sam's blackmail scheme has backfired but the threat of him will remain for some time.

Leslie will remain married to Sam until she finally files for divorce after learning that her son too has been...interfered with. By this time Mac will have been medically discharged from the Air Force due to his mental health. Again, Leslie's missive to Doris does not reflect that reality either.

Chapter 19
Doomed From the Beginning

It was doomed from the beginning. That would be easy for Doris to say and she could then simply be done with it. The future facts and events that would end up in full public view, would easily back up her statement. It would be simpler, but not the truth.

It is difficult for Doris to say that they were in love. Their relationship is going to cost her a great deal, but she believed, still believes, they were in love. The integrity of their marriage took several major hits early on. Doris and Gary will not live happily ever after.

Doris cannot with certainty state that their first child was planned. If she was, it wasn't Doris who did the planning. In the years that they knew each other, children were never discussed. About a week before their March wedding, Doris and Gary were together again for the first time. And, for the first time, Gary did not use a condom. At that moment what was more startling for Doris was that it appeared that Gary had learned a bit more about intercourse during their forced separation. So close to the wedding, she did not want to entertain the reality of her suspicions.

The truth would be known about halfway through the pregnancy—he'd had at least one interaction with a set of twins that he worked with. She would find this out after Gary introduced the set to her, later telling her that he'd been in bed with them. Together or separately, Doris doesn't know, and Doris does not care to ask. It would turn out to be only one of the many things that Doris did not know about her husband. For instance, she did not know how he came to enlist in the Air Force just a few years before they were to meet in Germany.

Men were drafted for the Vietnam War.[16] The draft began in 1964. Gary turned 18 in December of that year. One of the ways to avoid being drafted was to be enrolled in college. Gary was attending his first year at the University of Hawaii and, as the story told Doris goes, he became addicted to bridge.

Playing the card game 24/7 had left him little time to attend his classes. As a consequence, Gary found himself facing the Vietnam draft as he was notified that he would be facing expulsion by the end of that school year. Doris was to find out that he not only did not tell his parents that he was being expelled, but he joined the Air Force to avoid both their ire and the probability of being drafted into the Army.

His testing with the Air Force allowed him to be placed as a weather observer. By signing up with the Air Force, in 1965, he likely avoided potential infantry service on the front lines. After his basic training, he was trained in his specialty, asking for and receiving his first assignment in Germany.

The other way men kept from being assigned to Vietnam was to get married. There were so many men marrying to avoid the draft that by the 26th of August 1965, Lyndon Baines Johnson declared that not only must the military man be married, he must now also be a father.[17]

By asking for an overseas assignment to Germany directly from his training as a weather observer, Gary lessened the probability of

---

[16] https://thevietnamwar.info/vietnam-war-draft/
[17] https://thevietnamwar.info/vietnam-war-draft/

landing in Vietnam as his next assignment. So, after having served overseas, his next assignment was stateside—March AFB in California.

Riverside became their residence after they married in March of 1970. Doris would give birth to their daughter around Thanksgiving of the same year, while they lived in Illinois as Gary completed his advanced training. His first assignment, as a newly trained weather forecaster, would be Offutt A.F.B., Nebraska.

In 1973 a son was born at the base hospital. Gary would still be attached to the Global Severe Weather Central group when he left the Air Force in 1976. The draft ended in 1973 and the war itself in 1975. Gary left the Air Force never touching the soil of Viet Nam. Which makes his obituary rather interesting for what it says and what it doesn't say.

The inscribed "Special Operations," may refer to his time at Offutt when he served as a global weather forecaster. Doris doesn't know with certainty. However, after a bit more research online, she finds out that anyone who served during the time period of this war is able to have the war referenced on their gravestone, even if they never faced combat or served directly in Vietnam.[18]

Doris sits here, shaking her head, there is a sadness that is deeply felt. So much potential, so much he could have legitimately accomplished had he maintained his integrity. The obituary listed below is filled with accomplishments that would likely never have existed, if it had not been for Doris.

What is not mentioned among these accomplishments is Grand Larceny. Felons should not be able to have firearms, but if you've

---

[18] (Reference: https://vetsbenefits.net/the-word-vietnam-on-va-headstones-and-markers-t198753.html)

got a wife who manages to get you one of the best lawyers in the area, it is possible that you'll be able to plead guilty and end up with this being expunged from the public record. And, if you've served in the military during the Vietnam War it is possible for you to never serve prison time, but a period of probation.

In 1977 he was convicted of grand larceny and divorced Doris. By 1981 he is in Virginia graduating with a Bachelor's degree in Mathematics and Physics. Had he stayed in the Air Force, gotten his education while still serving, he could have achieved the same goals. Perhaps not as quickly. Perhaps with not as much fanfare, but perhaps with his original family intact.

Gary Riley Obituary Gary Tryer Riley 1946 - 2011 Gary Tryer Riley, 64, was born Dec. 6, 1946, in Orlando, Fla., and died Feb. 24, 2011, at Saint Alphonsus Regional Medical Center, in Boise, Id. A memorial service is scheduled for Thursday, March 3 at 1:30 p.m. in the Alden-Waggoner Funeral Chapel, Boise. The service will be followed by his interment at the Veterans Cemetery at 3 p.m. where he will receive full military honors. He was a Veteran of the Vietnam War who served from 1965 to 1976 in the U.S. Air Force as a meteorologist specializing in severe weather forecasting and came to Boise for work as Senior Meteorologist at Idaho Power, a venture lasting seven years. He has worked as Chief Meteorologist and

Senior Meteorologist and Deputy Project Manager for the Greek National Hail Suppression Project for five years; Vice President and Chief Atmospheric Scientist of Atmospherics Inc., Fresno, Calif., for 11 years; and Founder of Global Weather Connection. He earned a Master of Science degree in Atmospheric Science at the University of New York at Albany in December 1984. He earned his Bachelor of Science, Summa Cum Laude, in physics and mathematics from Longwood University, Farmville, Va., in 1981. He was an avid recreational target shooter, golfer, and an autocross and drag race driver and enthusiast; hobbies and interests shared with his son. He loved animals and enjoyed bird watching and volunteering at the local Humane Society. He was a loyal, loving, and supportive father whose thirst for knowledge and intellectual challenges was never quenched.[19]

---

[19] Published by Idaho Stateman on March 1, 2011

Pair Charged In Burglary

An employe and former employe of a Sarpy County truck stop have been charged in the Christmas burglary of the place.

Gary Riley, 30, of 7329 Edna Street, LaVista, was free on $2,500 bond Monday after being charged with burglary and conspiracy to commit burglary.

Glenn Angst, 29, of the same address, is still in Sarpy County jail under a $30,000 bond.

Riley has been an employe of Sapp Brothers at the corner of Interstate 80 and Nebraska 50, and Angst is a former employe.

Sarpy County deputy sheriffs said Riley had been on duty on Christmas when they were summoned to investigate a burglary at the truck stop.

A rear door had been forced in and a file cabinet jimmied, they said. Taken was about $20,000, about $9,000 in cash and the remainder checks.

Deputies learned from Sapp Brothers officials that Angst had been at the station during the evening, claiming he had run out of gas nearby.

The missing cash and checks were found at the pair's home.

4 January 1977, Omaha World Herald

Chapter 20
The Ending of the First Beginning

"Our Bodies, Ourselves: A Book By and For Women" was first published in 1971. In the 21st century, it can easily be accessed via the internet https://www.ourbodiesourselves.org/about-us/our-history/ . At the time of its publication, it was unprecedented. Never had such information been readily available to most women.[20] As the title states, it was by and for women.

The edition that landed in the hands of Doris was the second edition, published in 1973. Page 212 contains the section on tubal ligation, a form of sterilization. In January of 1973 Roe vs Wade becomes the law of the land. A second child is born in October of 1973 and immediately after that birthing, Doris undergoes sterilization.

Her determination to become sterile directly after the birth of her second child was met with some resistance. None of that resistance came from her husband. The doctors quiz her about her decision.

What if…the child she carried was another girl? In 1973 the sex could not be determined until the birth of the child.

What if…one of the children dies? The assumption is that you would want a replacement. So as Prince Harry put it, "Spare".

---

[20] The Boston Women's Health Book Collective, Our Bodies, Ourselves—A Book By and For Women. New York: A Touchstone Book Published by Simon and Schuster, 1973.

What if...she was to re-marry? Well, that question definitely gave her pause.

Doris understood their concern. She would turn 22 just prior to the birth of her son. Her whole adult life lay before her. It WAS a weighty decision. Yet, those concerns which were voiced did not reflect her concerns. What makes this insulting is that the reasons behind her decision were never requested either by the doctors, nor the husband who literally had to sign off on it. (Even after the Roe v Wade decision, apparently, he retained some kind of mining rights.)

The males did not seem to consider that when you decide to give birth you are ceding, at a minimum, two decades of your lifeline to the life you have chosen to carry. Additionally, our culture, our society want you totally responsible for these lives until your death. Divorce may not be pleasant, but abandonment is really frowned upon. Although plenty do walk away, and she understands why, Doris will not be one of them.

The other major consideration was birth control. None of the doctors suggested alternatives, and apparently, Gary felt no compulsion to use a condom. The pill came out in 1960, yet there were already warnings of side effects. Tubal ligation was the safest and surest way to ensure that she would no longer give birth. As for what if she re-married—if all her second husband needed was a breeding mare, such a marriage was not going to happen.

The very real possibility of rape had already been proven to Doris long ago. She never again wanted to face the choices involved concerning pregnancy. Another pregnancy would endanger the existing children, hindering her already handicapped ability to economically be responsible for them.

Doris was trapped. Doris felt trapped. Doris recognized the trap she was in. The trap all too many women have found themselves in since the beginning of time.

Doris is pretty certain that her marriage is not going to last much longer. She suspects that she is going to end up raising two kids on her own. A third child is totally out of the question. Something is off and she can't quite put her finger on it. Sure enough, about a year after their son is born, Gary decides they need a separation period. He deposits his family on Leslie's doorstep in Leavenworth, Kansas. (Leslie has finally divorced Sam by the time this happens.)

For about three months Doris will cook and clean and take care of the kids. Leslie rather likes having a housekeeper, so the fact that Gary hasn't left a dime for their support during this time period appears not to be a problem for her. One good thing that comes out of this fiasco is that Doris takes driving lessons and finally gets her license at the ripe old age of 23. Still not knowing what the hell is going on with her husband, Doris keeps asking, when he bothers to call, and all she gets is that he needs space.

Just as abruptly as they were dropped off, they were picked up and hauled back to Nebraska. Little to no notification. No explanation. However, during the drive back home, Gary tells her that there is someone he works with that he approached. Nothing happened. She had told him that she made it a rule not to date those she worked with. Oh, and by the way, he's decided not to re-enlist. While he hasn't notified the Air Force, and he won't have to for a couple of years, he is definitely not staying in.

Once back, Doris begins to question his decision. He seems focused on becoming a TV Weather personality. Don't you need a diploma for that? Why not remain in the Air Force, take advantage of your G.I. Bill and go after that diploma? She's met with a smirking smile that she interprets as his opinion regarding her opinions.

Around the same time period, the Resident Manager of their townhomes offered an assistant position to Doris, which she gratefully accepted. Gary always emphasized that he did not want her to seek employment outside the home. "No wife of mine...." She was determined to get some kind of experience under her belt. Now that she could drive, she would eventually land a full-time position as a switchboard operator at the Holiday Inn. She would work from 4 p.m. to midnight five days a week. Gary often wasn't home to cover for the kids, so they would stay with a couple across the street. The kids knew the couple; the couple knew the kids.

As the days come closer to his severance from the Air Force, his concern grows. So far, he's not landed a position. Seemingly out of nowhere, Glenn Angst shows up on their doorstep. The old roommates are reunited.

It is Glenn who initially gains employment at Sapp Brothers, and he would eventually secure a similar position for Gary. Doris does not know if Glenn gains employment elsewhere, simply quits, or is fired after Gary starts working for the truck stop. What Doris does know is that both men held their employer in contempt and that neither of them wanted to work for the organization. Rather than simply moving on to another gig the twosome somewhere along the line decide that robbery is the best answer to their situation.

Doris has no idea that any of this is going on. Stashing the stash in the basement of the townhome she and the kids were living in; suspicion fell on her as well. What would the kids have done with both parents jailed?

Doris received the call while working at the switchboard the night the police searched their townhome. The initial call was not from Gary but from her former boss, the resident manager. Trying to somewhat soften the blow to Doris she stated that she was sorry, but that she had to open the door because the police had a search warrant. Gary would call into the switchboard shortly after.

After arranging for the kids to remain with their babysitters overnight, Doris proceeded to make a series of calls that would ensure that Gary would be well-represented and that bail money would be available. And for those of you lucky enough not to have experienced a search of your home...the reminders are everywhere. The police did not ransack the place but everything was just placed back slightly off, slight reminders that someone else has been through your privacy. She spent what remained of that night alone and sobbing.

The only time that Doris ever received an apology from Gary about anything was just after she got him bailed out. Once and only once he said a single, "I'm sorry." Sometime later he would mention that she shouldn't be so hard on Glenn because he did not implicate her in the robbery. Doris was simply too stunned to reply.

I am beginning to lose patience with Doris. I am wanting to kick her ass into action. Enough already! Move on! And then I remind myself to remember what it is like to be blown by so very many winds that were neither sought nor understood. So many winds that kept attempting to blow her off her feet and down into a ravine she did not want to land in. I remind myself that it was the thought of two kids that kept her on her feet, leaning into those winds. It wasn't a matter of choice...she couldn't fall. She couldn't fail.

So far most of what has occurred in her life Doris has not directly initiated. That's about to change and the change is not good. She will manage to stabilize the kids after Gary leaves to live in Virginia, still working through his court-ordered parole, with the parents that he had purposely left when joining the Air Force all those years ago.

Since Doris was still on good terms with her former boss who was still the Resident Manager, the little family of three was able to move into a smaller townhome just a couple of blocks from where they were. The kids would still be in familiar surroundings, attending the same elementary, and the only familiar face that would be missing would be their father's.

For about a year the family of three will create a new stability, then there will be a choice presented and she will make the wrong decision.

Chapter 21
The Sin Of The Mother

"It's not what I am underneath but what I do that defines me."

Batman Begins

What you do with the seeds you are given, what you determine, what intent you have, will yield, will create, will produce a moment in time with ramifications for all future moments. Reap wisely, plant with care and above all, nurture that integrity of intent.

I failed my children. In a single decision, I failed them. I'll not lay this at the feet of Doris. I'll not lay this at the feet of the child that gave birth to children. It's time the third person is dropped. It's time to discuss the sin of the mother.

Things may appear to be going okay but I have less than a dollar left every pay period. I've never been on my own and the learning curve hasn't let up since the divorce. I am tired and still off balance. I am all too aware that all it's going to take is for someone to get sick, for the car to break down, for me to get in an accident and the entire house of cards collapses.

While it is true that Leslie is still in Kansas and that the group could gather there, I do not want my children in that close proximity to my mother. I do not want to be in that close proximity to my mother. Religion has returned to her life and she would have the children and I was absorbed by it. So, when less than a year after the divorce, Gary once again makes an appearance....

"Come to Virginia," he says.

You won't have to work unless you want to. My parent's house is big enough for all of us. The kids will get to know their grandparents. I'm starting college in the fall and it will be good to be a family again. The military still owes me a free move, so all the household items can be moved at no charge. If it doesn't work out, I'll pay for the return trip. As one of the employers I would end up working for in Virginia continuously put it: "You never learn."

"You Never Learn" was the owner of the restaurant I would work at, off and on, for over a year. The chef was from Hong Kong and I learned a great deal observing him when I could. He would carve the most wonderful birds from carrots. The food was great and the tips were reasonable. There were also two factory jobs.

In the electrical assembly position, I would work the late evening and graveyard shifts. This is when I learned to file for unemployment for the first and last time in my life. The layoffs were frequent and never far between. Two months of work might be followed by two months of lay off, which is why I sought additional employment. Often, I would be working two jobs trying desperately to keep our little household afloat.

As a sewing machine operator, I was part of the production line that produced men's velour shirts. You could always tell what color I was working on from the tissues that I was constantly blowing my nose with, even as I wore the masks that were mandated. To this day I have a distinct dislike for the material. I learned all about quotas and quality controls.

From both factory positions, I learned to appreciate protecting my hands. As an electrical assembler, I needed to avoid the plunge of the stamp that came down to seal the computer part I would be heat welding. At first, my fingers would become sore and sometimes blisters would form, so often they would be taped to protect them. Even more caution and focus were needed while operating the sewing machine. To this day I am amazed that I didn't lose a digit or two, or somehow damage nerves or tendons.

I was a good worker—always showed up and always just did my job. Apparently, the only job that Gary would consider was going to college full-time on his G.I. Bill. His parents had bought him a slightly used blue sports car so he could get back and forth to his classes. At least he and the kids were stabilized.

I soon found out that the $200 a month monetary support the kids were receiving was coming out of his grandmother's retirement account, and since the kids and I were staying there, rent-free, the money was expected to be given back so that they could re-send it each month. Gary was on parole after all, and it just wouldn't do for him to be considered behind on his child support. I quickly figured out why Gary left his parents behind.

His father, Paul, was something of a bantam rooster. A small strutting little man who had his wife, Glema, completely under his control. As a consequence, there was a very real pecking order in their house. I was quickly made aware of my place as Glema made her expectations of me known. It would be she who would arrange for my electrical assembly position at the company she was the Human Resource Secretary for.

Paul, who was retired from both the Air Force and the local school system, spent the majority of his days killing things with his dogs. Squirrel is not something I recommend and deer is difficult to prepare properly.

Paul and Glema had fully placed the blame for their son's thievery on Gary's buddy Glenn. Gary was just a victim of circumstance in their view of things. Me, well I was just someone that their son had married and wasn't it great they now had grandchildren!

I made the decision to work for wages, and to move into a place of our own shortly after we arrived. If I was going to have to work for a household, it was going to be my household. Being penniless was not an advantage in this situation, or any situation if you ponder it.

It took a few months but enough was finally accumulated for the four of us to attain our own walls. About half a year later, for some damn reason, I decided Gary and I needed to be married again. Dumb move number two! This decision was aided and abetted by members of the church group that my mother had determined needed to check in on me. Heaven forbids I should continue to be living in sin!

It was but a month after this second exchange of vows that Gary was telling me that he couldn't sleep with the mother of his two children. He thought I'd be okay with him telling me that he was in love with a woman even younger than I was and who was everything I could have been if I had somehow garnered access to education. He thought that this was okay because he wasn't sleeping with her. Apparently, he was certain that since he wasn't sleeping with her, and he was being up front and honest with me regarding his feelings that I would be okay with it.

When I said we were leaving his first response was to ask if I couldn't just stay a bit longer and pay some more of the bills. As the kids and I were leaving he let me know how relieved he was that we would be living with my mother in Kansas because he knew the kids would be taken care of. It appears his memory of my childhood must have failed him at about the same time he lost track of his moral compass. There was no logic to this world I had foolishly chosen to enter.

Luckily, I was more pissed than broken at that time. Anger literally drives me and the kids from Virginia to Kansas. I have to say, it took a lot for me to stop loving.

For the record…. If what you love is what you blame for your mistakes, you are definitely not thinking straight!

Chapter 22
The Ending Of What Should Not Have Begun

The kids were not the same kids I left the Midwest with, and I wasn't the same woman. As my anger ran out of gas, I began to more clearly understand the damage done. The kids and I no longer had even our household goods as their father had promised. We would be starting from scratch.

If I had been more stable at this time, I might have been more conscious of the silence in the back seat as I drove back. The damage done would not become apparent for about a decade, but both kids are subdued and overly compliant. They'll make up for that compliancy when they reach their teens. The unaddressed pain of a child grows as they do, as many who have been a child will attest.

We were lucky that my mother and grandmother were living together by this time. Grandmother had been living with her sister in Kansas City after retiring from Lockheed in California. As was par for the course with the two, Leslie had her story as to how the two ended up living together and Lynnette had her version of the event.

Leslie's story was that Lynnette and her sister got into a squabble and Lynnette decided to move out of Rose's house in Kansas City and move in with her daughter in Leavenworth. Lynnette said that she moved in with her daughter because Leslie was having difficulty financially. A bit of both is likely the truth. As far as the kids and I were concerned, the arrangement meant that they would be looked after while their mother got her act together. They, at least, would be provided some measure of stability after the chaos their parents had unleashed.

It would take three months before I would be able to file for a divorce in the state of Kansas. Since Gary and I had remarried in Virginia, Gary was off the hook for child support. I grabbed the first job I could and began the process of getting us dug out and on our feet again. The lawyer had to be paid, and the agreement with my mother and grandmother was that I pay one-third of the household expenses. During this time period, I served my little family of three first as a hotel auditor, later to be placed in charge of the reservation system.

Somehow, in little more than a year, the kids and I would be back in our old hood. Luckily, my ex-boss was still the Resident Manager. Luckily, their old childcare providers were still available and they would be returning to the elementary they had previously been attending. Luckily, I still was in the good graces of the management of the hotel I had previously worked at.

I continued my career of economic necessity by taking whatever job presented itself, always on the lookout for better insurance, pay, and hours. Consideration was not given to anything other than these qualifiers. What I wanted to do, or was inclined to learn held no sway. I was determined.

There was one thing that almost took me to my knees. While in her early teens, my daughter will tell me of her molestation by her paternal grandfather during the time we were in Virginia. I can't say what I said because it is still like a mist, a shock that hit so deeply that I felt suspended. She *seemed* okay with my response but I was numb for some time after. Then came the tears, sobs. She didn't witness that. She didn't need my pain on top of her own.

But we can't prevent that, can we?

What Does This Woman Want

To be able to hold my children, without the constant burden of their lives, when I have yet the self-realization of the capacity, I may have to govern my own.

To be able to marry, without the constant reminder of whose property I have become, when I have yet the scale on which to weigh my own worth.

To be able to stand alone, without the constant fear of loneliness, due to a society which has proclaimed me incomplete without a male by my side.

To be capable of completed action, without the constant fear of failure, which in turn, due to my sex, is not only condoned, but expected.

To be able to stand, human in form, with full understanding of that humanity, and the knowledge and strength derived therein.

I want to fully breathe, knowing the amount of air in which I am capable of survival, without this castration of my brain and body being the end result.

Chapter 23
Predators And Opportunity

The damage done when a child is used, is like a dog being kicked or a glass thrown to the ground. The instant it happens; the betrayal leaves its mark. These marks may or may not be physically visible, but lost trust is one definite outcome. When you lose trust, you know fear.

It will reside within the individual. It will reside within the child, the child that is not going to be fully developed physically or psychologically until their late teens, or early twenties. The targeted abuse will interfere with the healthy development and maintenance of boundaries. The potential for balanced relationships often spirals out of kilter. When this happens only the imbalance of the individual will be on full display, not the cause, not the abuser whose damage the spirit still fights. Believing in love, believing you are loved, is healing. It is as healing as it can be damaging when trust is broken.

As a young victim, the excuse I gave myself was that my abuse only occurred because I was not genetically related to the abuser. I told myself that this had to be the only reason this harm had come my way. I had done nothing to deserve such treatment, so this disparity of blood relation was what I told myself was the culprit. Believing that if Sam were not the Father-not-Father, believing that if I had been his genetic offspring, he would not have betrayed me.

My ignorance of my personal situation, not fully understanding that child sexual abuse is so prevalent, left my kids vulnerable. The statistics are damning.[21] I thought she was safe with his father because they were blood. I did not understand that "Child sex offenders are typically not strangers."[22] **I did not understand that when opportunity knocks the predator will pounce on the vulnerable.** There are so many assumptions that are made.

Children are flexible. Children bounce back quickly. They'll be okay. They'll get over it. It's like a bone, it will mend. They'll still walk, they'll still talk, they'll still…be angry. This anger is melded to our bones by the initial fear, the initial betrayal.

Do you know that one of the beliefs often held by child sexual abusers is that taking advantage of someone who is vulnerable, weaker than they are doesn't hurt them? According to a study of child sex offenders by Ruth Mann and colleagues in 2005, the first belief is that 'Sex with children is harmless,' and the second is the 'Children actively provoke adults to have sex with them.'*"[23] Lacking empathy for the child, lacking empathy for the victim, the predator may believe the child seduces them. And, "While sexual attraction to children is a risk factor for sexually offending against children, an even bigger risk factor is an individual's belief system.*"[24] As they hold these beliefs, they demand silence.

Silence is not required if what you do is honorable. Silence is not required unless it is apparent that the child does not want to accept abusive attentions. Silence is only required of the vulnerable.

---

[21] https://victimsofcrime.org/child-sexual-abuse-statistics/
[22] Julia Shaw, "EVIL—The Science Behind Humanity's Dark Side," (New York: Abrams Press, 2019) page number 176
[23] Julia Shaw, "EVIL—The Science Behind Humanity's Dark Side," (New York: Abrams Press, 2019) page number 175-176
[24] Julia Shaw, "EVIL—The Science Behind Humanity's Dark Side," (New York: Abrams Press, 2019) page number 175

If you confide what has happened to you, it is not uncommon to become enveloped in yet another type of silence. This silence is so heavy because the weight of it attempts to keep you silent once more. It compounds the damage done by the predator.

"Okay, now you've said it, forget it!"

When you out your predator, you out those that our culture expects to protect you. Some will not get past their self and culturally inflicted guilt because of what has happened to you. I know it has taken me years to come to understand that while I was not directly responsible for my daughter's abuse, I did not protect her from it. It has also taken me years to come to understand that while I did not protect her from it, had I known it was a possibility, I would have done all I could to keep her from that pain. I have forgiven myself, hopefully someday she will forgive me.

For scars to heal they must be cleansed and gently gathered together to form the safe space from which to heal the spirit. A safe space cannot be a silent space.

Others are often reluctant to hear that this has happened. Some don't want to hear because to know that it can happen to you means it could happen to them. Perhaps they are reluctant to perceive what may be their part in allowing the abuser access to you. In some cases, you may find the abuser was abusing them as well. These things seldom involve one victim.

It's like scenes of war that no one wants to interact with. The pain you have received; some will not want you to share with them. They may know your attacker and they may have a desire not to believe. I know how strong that desire to deny that pain is.

When I pushed Leslie to tell Lynnette about the abuse, Leslie warned me that I might not like the reaction from her. Leslie was at least partially correct. My grandmother was born just as the 1900's started. Even though her mother, my great-grandmother Bessie, was a suffragette, the right to vote is not on equal footing with the stigma of rape.

"No, not in my family."

Another myth is that it is a pedophile who abuses. "Not all child sex offenders are paedophiles, and not all paedophiles are child sex offenders."[25] While there is a certain percentage of the population of the world that have a physical response to children, most do not rape. Just like the rest of the human species, most do not rape. Most do not rape, but those that do, tend to do so serially. Most likely there is more than one victim.

A rapist is not some creep out there that can't control their sexuality. The rapist is not someone who is so overcome with their own sexual urges that they must force someone. Might providing you the opportunity to do harm, does not make you powerful. The ability to take will never trump the ability to give, but that is not how they experience the world.

A rapist's mind is Sam stating he won't penetrate because he wants to protect me from pregnancy. He knew he was sterile. He decided to be shamed because he would never genetically reproduce. He believed that because he could not reproduce, could not show that he was capable of reproduction, the world considered him a lesser man. He needed me to reflect a belief that he was capable of impregnation. He needed the world to see him as the genetic father of the two children he adopted.

---

[25] Julia Shaw, "EVIL—The Science Behind Humanity's Dark Side," (New York: Abrams Press, 2019) page number 175

In my teens, he began telling me that he was training me to be a good wife. Whatever the hell that is. You don't need a superiority complex built if you don't believe you need to build one.

Might presents a power of opportunity. Do you choose to take because you are able to? Do you choose to give, to protect, to elevate because of this opportunity?

The Victim Speaks

It is the reality of it,
It is knowing it can happen again and again,
And yet again.

It is the violence, the finality of the powerlessness.
The sneer, the look, the hate.

It is the guilt, the shame, the fear—which they will not accept,
Needing to force it back on you.

You, who have been violated.
You, who have been beaten.
You are to bear their guilt.

Your anger is disallowed.
You carry their shame and their fear and
You remain silent.

We instill it in our daughters. Silence,
Which teaches our sons, might
Gave you the right.

There are no words to say, that they will hear. Until,
We are silent no more.

Chapter 24

Finally....

The middle of January in the Midwest is about what you'd expect. Snow fell all through the early morning and we are being hammered again late this afternoon. The temperatures are to be sub-zero for the full week. Blizzards are definitely on our horizon, as winds are expected to exceed 40 m.p.h. Schools are scheduled to be closed. Across the border, the Republican primary is scheduled for Tuesday in the middle of all this. Nebraska, The Good Life....

When I began, I did not consider that I would end this writing the same month, a year later. The journey into my childhood has run its course. The story is told. Journeys have unexpected developments. While digging into the past enlightens the present, acknowledging the past creates new insights as you seek to express the truth of what you've found.

One insight I would like to share is that this aligning of the memory, the process of assimilating the history, unveils new patterns that a child would never have comprehended. What the child could not fathom, the adult can see far more clearly in this present day. I encourage you to write of your childhood. Write the memoir. If nothing else, make it a love letter to yourself. Self-love is the basis of all love—the heart cannot beat without the will to live. Please live.

As I approach my 73rd year of life, there is much that has changed regarding child abuse. In the 21st Century, I would likely have spoken to a teacher or to a librarian. I would likely have called any number of crisis lines. The books in the library, the conversations on the internet, the media all would have fed me the information I so desperately needed. The information, the support, the guidance that Doris so desperately needed. It is very difficult to act if you do not know who to call, how to call, how you might ensure your own safety. Yet….

Not a day goes by that I do not hear of another victim, another child that has been betrayed, used. Not a day goes by that I do not hear of the predator's abuse. Not a day goes by that I do not know the sorrow of realizing that what we are hearing is only a few voices of many who have not spoken or been spoken for.

It doesn't matter if you are one of the multitudes who have suffered. It doesn't matter whether the abuse you are subjected to is somehow more or somehow less than someone else. It doesn't matter that you are not going to be the last victim. What matters is how we interact with what has happened, what may be happening, what we will understand to be happening every day for the rest of our lives.

Every life is important. Every life story truly told is important. Every effort we make toward our own liberation is important. Every step we determine to take toward examining ourselves and our societies, we strengthen our resolve. Every time we pray, swear, curse, and cry out we verify the necessity of our existence. Every time, each and every time, we leave a mark upon this world that is needed and necessary! This world needs our voices, our strength, our compassionate understanding of human frailty.

My life began through the eyes of Doris and it is with her eyes I will always view this world.

Dearest Wild Thing,

I remember.

DLS, January 2024

A Sermon for Our Souls

There are not enough tears for the sadness of this world.

Our systems fail, all logic fails, events are rarely foreseen.
We fear attachment to anything, knowing it provides fodder for the
next assault.

The calluses are many, the scars…some, never heal.
I bleed as I continue to weep.
The patterns repeat.

The dam constructed does not stop the flow.
The barrier does not hold back the tides.
We prevail and assail and are overwhelmed.

There will never be enough tears for the sadness of our world.

They are at the source of what we encounter.
Not the cause of what is outside our realm of control.
They are the product of our labors.

Our tears are but the sweat of a heart still beating—still whole.

Part 2:
The Sins Of The Mothers

The Status Quo

It is a world in which everyone knows
What they are witnessing.
It is a knowledge gained. It was
Something else which was sought.

Lights, which show bright, reveal
Too many unlit corners.
Seeking truth, you find nothing other
Than what you fought.

The responsibility falls heavily upon our shoulders.
Bent and twisted, we simply shrug
As Pilate washes his hands
Of the murderous plot.

Delusion is not
An instantaneous moment,
It is a lifetime of trying to disavow
What you have found.

Introduction
The Sins Of The Mothers

Sam threatened that if I spoke of what he was doing, my mother, my brother, my grandmother, and even my dog would die. As a child, I believed that my family would die if I spoke of what he was doing, while simultaneously being taught that I was to blame for what he was doing. The "I am hurting you because you made me hurt you but you can't stop me from hurting you," is a theme park I visited way too many times as a child.

If you do not speak of the abuse, the abuse will continue, and it is likely that it will escalate, morph over time. This affliction is like addiction, and addictions do not naturally recede but seek amplification. As in all forms of power plays, the instigator seeks to ever expand their domain. When you don't believe in your own personal power, power over others is an ever-expanding need.

If you do speak of it, if you do "out" your abuser, there are repercussions attached to that choice as well. The ramifications of testifying to the death of trust in a family are not to be taken lightly. Your abuser is likely to attempt to turn the spotlight of blame on you. You may be a child, totally blameless, but the family unit may come to see you as somehow complicit.

The longer the abuse goes unreported the more likely they are to see you as somehow benefitting from an NDA—a non-disclosure agreement they, or your abuser, might accuse you of having made. If you find yourself facing this situation, understand that there are scientifically valid, centuries-old legal reasons why a minor cannot enter a legal contract without adult consent.[26]

The Sins of the Mothers is primarily based on at least six years of written correspondence between myself, my mother, and my maternal grandmother. The inclusion of this correspondence provides a window into some of the twists and turns that may be encountered.

What will cross the path of the communications here are our ever-present separate visions, remembrances of jointly experienced pasts. The events being discussed are about three to four decades old when they are written about. The remembering of more than one person will not coincide in all areas. That's a given.

My abuse is never doubted. No one doubts the abuse occurred. Your case may be different. You may not be believed. That is a road I never traveled except in my initial fears. Fears, that are all too valid in so many other instances, for so many other victims. You may also find that some will even attest to being suspicious that this was occurring.

I cannot say that being believed made any of the repercussions any easier. I definitely can say that I have never regretted outing my abuser. I can also definitely say to you that I do not in any way mean to infer that you MUST. Always, always, always, I wish you safety first and foremost, at all times.

---

[26] https://www.upcounsel.com/minors-and-contracts

The Word "Sin"

"Let's look at the word 'sin.' It comes from the Greek and was a term used in archery. When an archer missed the mark, he was said to have 'sinned.' That's all it means: to miss the mark. The Bible tells us that the wages of sin is death. When you see that the original contest was war that meant that an archer who consistently missed his target was likely to get killed. So, in that sense, the statement is true. But through poor translations we have come to associate the word 'sin' with guilt and condemnation.[27]"

---

[27] Terry Cole-Whittaker, "What You Think of Me is None of My Business", (A Jove Book- mass marketing addition, published by Berkley, an imprint of Penguin Random House LLC, April 1988) (Copyright 1979 by Terry Cole-Whittaker). Page number 120-121

Chapter 1
How It Began

A Morning Prayer

May thought of duty not weigh so heavily upon my heart, that I might find joy in the act of its completion.

May I always remember that "duty" is another word for need, and that need evolves as a sign of growth.

May I always be strong enough to act, for all who have need of me.

May I with grace proceed with clarity and purpose, in the service of those about me.

Allow me to act knowing their growth is mine as well.

Let the joy be for all when all have gained.

In the spring of 1992, our country was riveted by Rodney King's declaration: "Can we all just get along." The L.A. riots were torched by the verdicts against four Los Angeles police officers videotaped in the act of brutally beating King, a black man, during arrest. Shortly after they were acquitted on the 4th of April, the violence began and did not fully end for over a week. There would be more than 12,000 arrests and 63 deaths. In mostly south-central

Los Angeles, the damage to property would grow to exceed a billion dollars.[28]

Leslie was up for a visit from Leavenworth. For some time, I had been attempting to get an explanation as to why she remained married to Sam for as long as she did. I was 16 when Gary and I met her as she got off work at the Lansing Hospital in Germany. She divorced Sam after I had given birth to her second grandchild. Even though it had been over 25 years, it always haunted me that she had remained married to him.

A few years before, she had confided in me that she feared I would no longer trust her because of what had happened. She was right to be fearful, but to combat it I needed answers. Answers that neither she nor Mac were willing to supply.

We're sitting out back. The weather is pleasant. As I keep prodding, she keeps dodging. After a rather deafening few minutes of silence, she flatly informs me that she didn't sleep with Sam after she found out. I never thought of her sex life with him and was both confused and angered by the remark. Was some innuendo being made?

We move indoors to the kitchen table. I don't remember how the riots came up, but we are now in an increasingly emotionally charged conversation concerning them. Leslie is going on and on about the fires and looting that took place.

"What kind of people burn down their own neighborhoods?"

"People who don't believe they have anything left to lose."

---

[28] 1992 Los Angeles riots - Wikipedia
Los Angeles Riots of 1992 | Summary, Deaths, & Facts | Britannica

She looks up at me and glaringly pronounces, "You don't even stand up for your own race!"

Where the hell did THAT come from?

Neither of us was cognizant of what was to come to pass within a year's time. After trying to communicate with her and my brother for years about the damage we all suffered, I'd come to the place where I didn't have anything left to lose.

Simply put, I'd had enough of their passive aggression, their pot shots at me. I'd had enough of their ignoring my pain, their pain, our pain. Did we truly all mean so little to each other, that we could not discuss our common antagonist and the damage that had been done? Perhaps we might clarify for each other inconsistences such as the question that remained unanswered regarding why she remained married to Sam? Why were they being so defensive?

There had been a couple of occasions, over the years, when my grandmother had come close to asking me directly if I was being abused by Sam. The questions were vague, like questions of how someone is doing that we all ask each other. Perhaps I was imagining that she was asking about that issue in particular. All I knew was that I always felt as if I had lied...I did lie.

On more than one occasion I had been told to tell Grandmother. Leslie always implied that Lynnette's reaction was not going to be what I thought it would be. I'm not certain what she thought I thought it would be, but apparently it wasn't going to be positive for me.

At the age of 42, I lost patience with Leslie. I mailed her a note informing her that she either opened up to Lynnette or we would not be coming down to Leavenworth, and she would have to supply the reason as to why.

The correspondence may have been addressed to Leslie, but the response to that mailing came from Lynnette. What ensued was not desired and was certainly not expected, but it was horribly enlightening. There are times in life that you wonder…do you really want to learn, to know, to ponder further? There are also times in life when you regret, not what you've done but what you've decided not to do. There were other paths that might have been taken. Other paths that could have been taken by me, by them, by us.

Salve should not be presented on wounds not given the opportunity to be cleansed. Wounds that are not acknowledged continue to acknowledge themselves. The poison goes deeper; the damage becomes more pronounced. None of us are going to end up looking like the picture-perfected Dorian Gray.[29] What goes into the closet, does not stay in the closet. Sooner or later, someone or something opens that door no matter how many locks are put in place.

Why did I wait until my 40s? I had hoped they would work out their conflicts, conflicts that they would separately attempt to put me in the middle of, by one complaining of the actions or words of the other. In this scenario, I held the position of a trusted servant, or so it seemed to me. A confidant of sorts, I was akin to the United Nations and I held about as much power to get things settled.

Again, why did I wait until my 40s? A child cannot mature fast enough, especially when their very ability to stand alone has been compromised. First you are handicapped, then when you appear handicapped, you're told to be appreciative of the crutches they've given you just so you can somehow walk that last mile for them. Some of us are more resilient than others. The ramifications of abuse

---

[29] Dorian Gray (character) - Wikipedia
https://www.britannica.com/topic/The-Picture-of-Dorian-Gray-novel-by-Wilde

are felt past childhood and infect the entire family unit. "Family patterns are passed down through the generations without conscious awareness, and the dysfunctional dynamics that occur in one generation contain symptoms that reverberate horizontally across generations and vertically from one generation to the next. *"[30]

An empty-nester at 42, most of my life had been a roller coaster that I had little choice in riding. What choices were available to me were determined primarily by the actions others had taken. I was the one presented to all the sins around me—the family sin-eater. I was the cleanup crew. Totally true or not, it is how I felt. It seemed to be the role the family wanted me to fill.

"May thought of duty not way so heavily upon my heart that I might find joy in the act of its completion." This was the opening line of a poem I had written in my 20s. Little had changed in the two decades that had followed. My heart was heavy.

Love is not an excuse. Love is a responsibility, not a death sentence, not a life sentence, not a license to harm yourself or others. None of us are a given in anyone's life and what is given must be consistently earned. Love must be guarded and nurtured, as that is what the bedrock of love is. Why would it surprise us that love, when trust is broken, would be withdrawn and injured?

As is true for the word "love," the word "trust" is both a noun and a verb. You trust someone. You decide to trust someone. A trust is created between two parties. When the trust is broken, the agreement is broken. There are ramifications to breaking an

---

[30] Teresa Gil, "Women Who Were Sexually Abused as Children—Mothering, Resilience, and Protecting the Next Generation", (published by Rowman & Littlefield, an imprint of The Rowman & Littlefield Publishing Group, Inc., 2018). P.146

agreement. If you decide not to come to the table for arbitration, so be it.

Choices are made. Consequences follow.

Chapter 2
1993, It Begins

"August 1993

Dear Granddaughter,

I sit here reading the one sentence you wrote to your mother, dated on my birthday. That I should be told the TRUTH. What Truth or which Truth?

She thinks that what you referred to in the note is the fact that you were raped from the time you were about ten until you were about 16. That when she found out about it, she went to the Chaplin and to the authority that handles such things in the military and they told her that nothing could be done unless he was caught in the act. It seems that Gary was in on it in some way and that he and your mother did accuse him to his face and threatened him if he continued. I suspected all of this but did not know.

And what your mother has never told me but what had been plain to see all of her marriage to him is that she was really physically afraid of him. And she felt she could not turn to me in any way because I had always hated him and the sight of him. I suspected that he was abusing you…and there was something he was doing to your brother…what it was your mother never knew. Did he try to get your brother to rape you also and did your brother abuse you too? Neither Leslie nor I know but there seems to be a deep-seated hatred for him from you? What is the truth about that?

You know, if you are willing to admit it, that you are the love of my life, my first grandchild. Your Grandpa and I adored you and I still do. Your mother loves you dearly and is very proud of you. She came to your aid when and if she could. Just what has brought all this on?

Come on, let's face it. You have allowed something in the past to grow until you just had to open the wounds to drain the poison. We love you very much and hope that you will acknowledge that I have been told and I hope this Truth is the one you wrote about. If not please jog our memories so that your truth can come out.

I do and always will love you,

Grandmother"

The note was sent to Leslie. The opportunity was presented to Leslie. The path she chooses is not a wise one. As I will come to learn, the path she chooses is the one she's been trudging along on most of her adult life and she is not the only one of us partaking of the well-worn paths we have created for ourselves. Each generation affects other generations, just as each seed produced mutates for good or ill.

As I was not anticipating a 7-year long communique, I do not have a copy of my apparently mutiny instigating note. I was anticipating a phone call from Leslie. Grandmother is the letter writer. Grandmother and I had been regularly writing to each other since she taught me to write. So, rather than responding to me directly Leslie's decided to simply hand it over to Lynnette. Bad move for all involved.

In the meantime, there are a few bits of information in this response that are already sounding alarms. Grandmother and I have written to each other for most of my life, I know the tone of her writing and this is a tone I've never encountered before. Condescending. Never has she ever used that "voice."

"And she felt she could not *turn to me in any way because I had always hated him and the sight of him."* This is a bit confusing. If you wanted

someone to turn to, wouldn't someone who couldn't stand the person in the first place be the likely person to turn to?

I am certain that I did not mention Mac in my "one sentence" to Leslie. An attempted rape by my brother? What the hell have been the conversations between my mother and brother? I have a deep-seated hatred for my brother? How is it that Leslie does not know what happened between Sam and Mac? I know some things from personal experience, but she has not spoken with Mac? I should not be surprised, but I am.

What is this attempted rape that's just been thrown into the conversation? There was no attempted rape. There was the scenario where Sam was attempting to set me up for blackmail to keep me under his control, but there was nothing remotely corresponding to this accusation. Never.

Mac seldom came up in communications with my Grandmother. We weren't avoiding talking about him, he simply wasn't part of our conversations. This would be Leslie speaking.

I don't like my brother. I don't trust my brother. I don't hate my brother. Why is she throwing him under the bus like this? Why is Mac being brought up at all, and what is with this "We?"

Perhaps I can answer the "We" question. I did throw that gauntlet in Leslie's face, didn't I? Well, she's just thrown it right back at me. Lynnette is right about one thing, I had "…to open the wounds to drain the poison." After over 35 years, there's a lot of poison.

On the 15th of August, I composed and posted my reply to Lynnette. I received a phone call from her before she had received this mailing. Lynnette called around 6:30 in the evening, two days before she would receive my reply. I took notes as we spoke:

Did I get her letter?

Yes, I got the letter and one is in the mail. If not arriving in the mail today, probably tomorrow.

She had to pry it out of her.

The McBratney side.

She loves me.

She loves her daughter.

Leslie and I have agreed not to argue.

Tom sent her a birthday card which said 'Cheer Up, I could have been twins!'

She suspected this had happened.

She begged Leslie not to marry him.

I said I'd wish Leslie would write.

I asked if she'd found the card that was with the raspberry tea.

(I also have written a note that I don't think Leslie was at home when she called.)

The games began with Leslie not directly responding. Then the condescending voice of the written response from Lynnette set off alarms. With Grandmother phoning me, one face is given to Leslie and another face is presented to me. Talking behind each other's back, particularly at this point, is not helping the situation. She may love me and she may love her daughter but by doing this she has undermined us both.

She states that Leslie and she have agreed not to argue. This is a reoccurring theme. Agreeing not to argue is akin to stating that they have decided not to discuss this. This also infers that there is already disagreement. What are they in disagreement about that they have determined that they cannot discuss? What is of such importance to both of them that such an arrangement is agreed to?

"The McBratney Side," is yet another theme that is played throughout. Lynnette almost had me buying into this so, it would not be surprising to pick up on anything that would fit this version of the world she's fed herself and now, me. It's not helpful. Who among us is qualified to get into the Genetics vs. The Environment debates? Another alarm is that the genetic similarities mentioned are all negatives.

If Leslie handed the note, or read the note to Lynnette why did Lynnette have to "…pry it out of her?"

My confusion is growing.

Chapter 3
Round One

If I had received the phone call prior to posting my response, this response would have been different in tone and content. Lynnette receives the letter, as shown below, on the 19th of August.

"15 August 1993

Grandmother,

I love and adore you also, which is why not being able to speak to you openly has caused me great pain these many years. There have been two times that you have asked me about Sam, and two times I have lied. Two times I have denied myself the opportunity to be held in the arms of the one person I have always known to love me with any consistency. There have been many times, during my childhood, when the thought of you kept me sane. There have been many times where the strength I have found has been but an imitation of what I felt your actions would be. I love Thee.

That it is you who have written, I am not surprised. How is it that I address a letter to her and I hear from you? Disappointment, in regards to my mother, is something I am far too use to. I waited all these years for her to talk to you. My heart believed that you and she had issues that the two of you needed to deal with, and when that happened, she would speak to you of this. Such has not been the case. I lost patience on your birthday.

I was faced with another trip to Kansas where I would spend the time trying to be with my Grandmother, avoiding a lot of potential conversations because you did not know of what had happened, and trying to avoid my brother and mother as much as possible. The older I've gotten the less I like them. If I'm going to spill my guts, I might as well go all the way....

Inform my mother that I lost my virginity closer to age 8, not age 10.

That she was physically afraid of him does not surprise me. I do not remember her having cuts, bruises, or being physically 'man-handled.' I do remember my brother and I having been treated thus. Also, until your letter, I have never heard her mention nor complain about such treatment. This is the first time I have heard this particular excuse. And yes, I consider it an excuse.

This is the first time I've heard about the military saying he had to be caught in the act. I knew that she claims to have gone to some military authorities, but the only one I remember meeting was some jerk of a Chaplin who was basically concerned that I was some type of street walker, or about to become such—this individual my mother left me alone with inferred that I led Sam on and should learn not to be so seductive.

For someone who was trying to get his ass in trouble, I find it amazing that she remained married to him—we got back from overseas in 1969. At age 16, the year was 1967. She did not divorce until 1973 or 1974. I fail to see how anything or anyone but herself dictated that she remains married to a man she knew had raped her daughter. Also, I don't believe I would respond to this daughter's questioning of that fact by supplying me with the much-needed information of how she didn't sleep with him during this time period!

She says she couldn't turn to you because you couldn't stand the sight of him—Thank God someone had some taste! I think we are somewhat closer to the truth here. My guess, and it is a guess, is that she didn't want to face you with this reality. Truth AND the consequences.

Last year I asked why she hadn't told you and her reply was: "Why don't you tell her?" My visit after that she told me she was going to write some kind of life-story about <u>herself</u>, which would help me to understand. I have not seen nor heard a word of it. Such has been the loving concern of my mother.

The wording of your letter leads me to believe that you have been told that this is some kind of new development with me—THIS IS NOT TRUE! I have been attempting conversations actively for some time with mother. I gave up on my brother about two years ago.

My brother seems to think that all his sister really needs to do is just get rid of all that anger. No problem, Bro, I'll just eliminate it with the evening's trash! Someone PLEASE do a reality check on these two. Neither he nor mother will sit still long enough to discuss this, or when and if it rarely occurs, they have major, major problems handling the conversation levels—but let us not forget that I, Yes, I am the one WITH THE PROBLEM. The last time I checked we all went through this, but I guess I'm just overly sensitive to abusive situations. It must be nice to be so thick- skinned as to be unaffected by something of this magnitude.

Since I don't feel like being fat, smoking and drinking to excess, and being in debt up to my ass—I guess I'll just have to resort to: talking, writing (re-read some of my poetry it is in there too), thinking, studying, and just generally trying to understand, and Yes, this type of activity can and does cause anger to arise for you to deal with and heal.

The big question is not my anger, but what happened to theirs?

I have received more loving, care, and shared understanding in one night from a room full of total strangers, than I have received my entire life from my brother and mother. For them, I guess, what happened to them and to me is of such importance that my brother feels that is it OK to have Sam in his home on several occasions. And mother seems to like to repeat to me about how when Sam asked her how I was, she replied: "I wouldn't go near that one if I were you." I really, really long to hear: "If you come near my kids, I'll kill you!" No, as always, it will be I who fights—even now.

My brother seems to like to repeat this particular myth: "Mom taught us how to survive." No, mother tried to teach us how to be good little victims so she'd never have to explain her inactions. Does the word 'neglect' ring a bell? Rape isn't all that happens in an incestuous household. I fit the stero-typical eldest, female child role like a glove. I can still remember the smell of cat shit in and on my clothing.

I have worked long and hard to get myself to this point. But the forgiving process cannot begin until someone states what he or she has done to be forgiven for.

I have an extremely hard time with an attitude, which dictates to her that she must tell her divorce lawyer to tell Sam's lawyer that he'd best not fight the divorce because both kids are willing to testify—long after the rapes have ceased and both kids are out of the nest. Has she ever told you why she initiated the proceeding? I threatened that she'd never see her grandchildren again. I was in my final months of pregnancy with my son when I got a call from my brother's first wife. She had my brother admitted to the psycho ward at Offutt because something had triggered a childhood memory. What was mother thinking, Grandmother? Was she going to bring Grandpa Sam over to visit my kids? There's more, but I'll leave the damage count here for the moment.

You know what is really tearing at my guts right now is how she readily abdicated her role of mother yet again to you. Then, she complains because I treat you that way.

Mother, get honest with yourself. It is the only way this can work. If you feel you are being honest, there is nothing more for us to discuss, because I am being as honest as I know how. Have no doubt that our relationship is on the line NOW. What a child of 8 to 16 years of age could not do, this 40-year-old adult is now prepared to do. If you will not nurture and protect me, have no doubt that I will.

Grandmother, should I sever ties with her, I will abide and fully understand if you determine it is necessary to sever your ties with me. It is my hope that all fully understand that we deal here with not one or two generations, but four. The neglect and betrayal of our children is not acceptable to our female line, and I will not set my daughter such an example.

Always with love and respect,"

"As long as you keep secrets and suppress information, you are fundamentally at war with yourself."[31] As Dr. Van Der Kolk notes, keeping silent carries a burden of tension that is not lightened over time. The longer you hold back the truth, the longer you carry this load of lies, the heavier your heart becomes. If the truth is being held back to protect another, it becomes doubly damaging. It damages not only you but if you are still attempting to maintain a relationship(s), it damages those relationships as well. It weakens all who know of the secret when the secret is being kept at the expense of other relationships, and ultimately that definitely includes your relationship with yourself.

One thing I would mention at this point is that going forward there will be little to no mention of Mac. What I did not tell Leslie at the time of Mac's hospitalization was that when he was triggered his wife told me that he pushed her down the stairs and that she had subsequently miscarried. I did not mention it to her because I could not, and still cannot, corroborate his soon-to-be ex's story. Did Leslie ever question Mac as to why he was hospitalized? He never spoke to me about this period of time, and once again, one of those conversations that should have happened could have brought healing to us all.

Meanwhile, Leslie's long-awaited letter has arrived.

---

[31] Bessel Van Der Kolk, M.D., "The Body Keeps the Score—Brain, Mind, and Body in the Healing of Trauma." (New York: Penguin Books, 2014) p. 235.

Chapter 4
Leslie's Letter

The 21st of August I journal....

"Still no response from Leslie. Not sure whether or not I should be even expecting one. My life feels like it's going up in smoke. Susan says that it is time for me to live for myself, yet we go back to her place and it is crammed full of teens. I've so much to do that I don't know what I <u>have</u> to do. Don't know that I have to necessarily do anything."

On the 28th Jay receives a call from GG. She asked for me and was weak-voiced in the beginning. Jay replies that I was out with friends. Grandmother then asked if I had received the letter from Leslie yet. The letter dated the 21st and postmarked the 23rd and then again, the 27th because the zip code is wrong, arrives....

"21 Aug 1993

Dearest Lynnette,

I don't know if you want to hear from me or not and I've always been a poor letter writer and communicate best face to face or by phone. But I am writing in hopes I can get you to understand some things but as to whether you even want to see me or talk to me is your decision. You will always be loved and welcome but I still will not force myself on you. Although we do not remember the past the same, I have always felt your pain.

The fact that you called me Leslie makes me realize your rejection of the woman you believe me to be.

I had a normal happy life until I was a teenager. I was surrounded by a loving family.

But as a teenager I became unsure I felt that even when I was thinner my senior year it didn't help because I was treated just the same. I wasn't popular or unpopular. I had friends in both ends of the rainbow. But I became very insecure and learned to use laughter against anything that hurt. I came to feel I never could be popular with the boys. I had friends who were male but they were just friends. Then I meet your Dad. Then a week after we were married, I went to Japan and back 5 months later and pregnant with you. Jim had stayed at Coronado Island and went to sea and Korea on an LSD (landing craft) shortly after I got back to California. You were 2 when he left the Navy and came to KC where I was with my parents. Mac was born 9 months later. We loved each other but there was a lot against the marriage so it failed. 1.) I had been an officer—he was a petty officer. 2.) The differences between were culture of the hills of West Virginia and urban Kansas. 3.) Alcohol.

Later after I got my divorce, I was to marry Charles. In many ways he was difficult to live with. Sometimes I think I only held on because I did not believe in divorce and to have a second one was very distasteful.

Of course, when you were 16 the shock came. You and Gary met me at the back of the ward as I got off at midnight and told me what had been going on since I first married Charles. I sent you to friends for the night. Gary made an appointment with the legal office and went with me. I was told that I could do nothing, as it would be hearsay. You would have to bring the charges—I don't know why you wouldn't. The chaplain I talk with would only say we should forgive him. That was a big help. I wrote your Grandmother to see if I could send you to her. You decided not to go.

When we returned to the States—he left for Thailand. You were married. So, things were confused and I had to face the future alone. When Charles returned Mac was a senior and I don't remember what really happened but it was Hell till he returned to Thailand. The divorce was delayed, as I had to have him out of the house before it could be filed. When I got him out finally.

He fought it and we finally had to tell him we would tell his lawyer the truth if he didn't give in when he finally did, I got it.

I have told Mother and if at any time you wish to come to see her you won't have to see me. I will get out of your way. Just tell her when you are coming and I'll leave.

Sincerely and with Love,

Mom

P.S. As my life has been bitter and I have only found peace thru the church. I will be there when you need me but I will not bother you unless invited."

No apology. Once again, no apology. Can you not just state that you are sorry?

It is interesting that the family shorthand for what happened to me is now being referred to as *"the truth."* What proves to be NOT the truth is:" I will not bother you unless invited."

That I had been raped by her husband for over a decade because she was not popular with the boys, was not a good thought. That she had not sought a divorce until six years after she knew of the abuse because she felt divorce was "distasteful," was not a good thought. That she had asked me to testify and that I would not, threw me into a blind rage. Even if this is one memory versus another, how could she even imagine that I would not have stood up in a court of law and stated the truth? Later, as referenced in Part I, I would gain written testimony from Gary that they never went to the military legal authorities.

This letter put a stake in my heart. Actually, this proves to be a rather poignant analogy. Because if my Mother's words became a stake, what I received next from my Grandmother can be perceived to be the sword that chopped off my head. Finally, the gloves come off. Snail-mail being what it is/was....

The envelope is dated 20 August 1993 the day prior to Leslie's?

"Dearest,

Your letter did not come until yesterday. I read it and gave it to your mother to read. I had already told her about our telephone talk. She was almost hysterical and we talked about an hour. I had known for years that she was jealous of our relationship but did not understand why she was. You are the dearest person in the world to me. She went back to work as soon as she could after you were born. And your grandpa and I devoted our lives to you. She was badly hurt and scarred by both of her marriages. When you were about fifteen months old, she took you out to visit your father, whose ship had come in to Coronado (probably misspelled). You had some lovely clothes such as a blue velvet coat and hood. You were really a little doll. I had had a windfall; I guess you could call it that. Anyway, my mother had died and she had an insurance policy and my dad divided the money from it among her five children. I bought a few things for the house such as an electric toaster. And I spent the rest of it on our grandchildren. Such as a coat and suit for your two cousins, one of which had just been born. I bought a very beautiful hand embroidered by the nuns, christening dress. I made her a white coat and hood. The best was not good enough for MY grandchildren. But it seemed to have impressed your Father for he seemed to think we had money so he came out of the Navy when his enlistment was up. Anyway, the marriage was a bust with him promising your mother and still expecting her to pay their way. They were in Rosedale and she was working at KU Med Center and was pregnant with your brother. Two weeks before your brother's birth she had to quit work and when she did your father moved out. She called us for she was broke and we brought her home again. She called him when she left for the hospital to give birth to your brother. He did come to her there and was with her when he was born. But they did not go back together although she would meet him somewhere. I just did not know. We took care of you kids for four months. We, your grandpa and I had devoted all our time to you two and we were invited to a big party. Your Aunt was going to take care of you two and we were looking forward to a good time. We went down town so I could buy a new dress and I found one I really liked. We got home just as a taxi came and your mother took you both and left to join your father. That was when they went to West Virginia. We did not hear from them for some time. The reason I am telling you this is because from the time of your birth until yesterday when your letter came your mother has been unable to confide in me. Now maybe I am to blame for that. I am sure all the blame is not on one side. The only times I remember quarreling with her was when I was living with you three and Sam was in Alaska and I would get angry with her because I felt that she should do part of the housework even though she was working.

Another thing she cannot help. Sometimes when I just look across the room at her, she looks so much like my Mother-in-law it is almost a shock. She is a McBratney thru and thru. And your mother's reactions to any problem have always been like hers. Not that mine were or are any better. It's just that they are mine.

If I had known what went on with Sam there would be at this time one less Sampson and your grandmother would either be hung or be in prison.

You surely think by now that I am being the lawyer for defense of my daughter. Not exactly.... But I do very much hope that you two can get together and clear this thing up. She says she will write you.

You have been a joy to me and I hurt when you hurt and I know it. All of my life I have tried to help those I love and would like this all to be settled before I die.

Remember I love both you and Jay very much.

GG"[32]

I had known for years that she was jealous of our relationship...." I am not quite sure how to interact with this. Turf war?

"The reason I am telling you this is because from the time of your birth until yesterday when your letter came your mother has been unable to confide in me." Okay, I know that's not true.

The McBratney resemblance? If she is being the defense lawyer for her daughter, her daughter needs a new lawyer.

---

[32] Please note that "GG" is a family reference for Great-Grandmother. Later you will also see the reference of "GGG." Great-Great-Grandmother.

Chapter 5
Round Two

The birthday card is postmarked 25 August 1993. "Having a daughter is like watching a rose as it slowly unfolds its petal to the sunlight, one by one." Inside the card, it reads: "Each birthday you celebrate brings even more beautiful reasons to love you and be grateful for you. Happy Birthday." It is signed: "Love Mom."

For the first time in my life, my grandmother sends nothing. This is very bizarre. Leslie, who quite often is late or forgets my birthday, remembers and Grandmother, who never has been late in over 40 years, sends nothing.

A few days later, postmarked the 31st, I received this notecard from Grandmother:

"Dear Lyn, [33]

Your note came yesterday. The only weekend Leslie will not be here is the 18th and the 19th. Any other time that you can come she will go away so that you will not be bothered by her, so come when you can but let us know so that she can be gone.

Please do this for me. Sit down and make two lists. One with all the things she has done that hurt you, the other list all she has done for you.

---

[33] I am certain that you have already figured out that except for legal matters and Part 1 of this book, I am rarely referred to as "Doris." I was referred to as "Lynnette" until my sophomore year of high school, when Grandmother Lynnette suggested that I refer to myself as "Lyn."

I saw my doctor last Thursday and had to have more tests. He called yesterday and I have to go see him today at 2:45. He is trying so hard to really take care of me but I am getting weaker all the time and I have become a walking pillbox.

My love to Jay. Keep some for yourself.

GG"

For whatever reason, I do not have a copy on file of the note she refers to having received from me. It is possible that she is still referring to the reply I had sent earlier. I know that during this time period, I was still very much upset by Leslie's letter, and now the concept of writing up the lists that Grandmother requested became very unsettling. I was having none of it....

"2 Sept 93

GG, you last letter came today. I had planned to come down the 3rd, but I feel this might be a bit too soon. I am sorry to hear of your medical problems, and do hope the doctor could give you a clean bill of health. Taking a lot of pills cannot be much fun, no matter how necessary they are deemed to be. It will not be necessary for Leslie to leave her own home should we come down. As to the lists you have requested....

It is becoming clearer and clearer that there is much both of you are not aware of. For instance, I have one of the symptoms common to many incest victims— memory lapses. This makes the accomplishing of the lists you have requested an impossible task for me to do with any accuracy. It has been my personal experience as a victim and as someone who has been certified as a crisis line counselor, worked as a facilitator in incest related group therapies, and after having done numerous papers, speeches, and at least 10 years of study on the problem, that the type of lists you have requested are not feasible in this situation. This is because these lists cannot possibly answer the question of: 'Even if someone gives you everything, how many times do they get to..."

Among victims of child sexual abuse, it is not at all uncommon to have memory problems. This phenomenon is similar to P.T.S.D. (Post Traumatic Stress Disorder), and many victims have been diagnosed as having this disorder. PTSD was first discovered with the Viet Nam vets. Even if there are good memories, they are mixed in with the bad. The mind, in its efforts to protect its sanity, is often not terribly selective. In other words, it often 'throws out' or 'represses' the good along with the bad.

I cannot, for instance, remember but a handful of classmates from grades 1-12. Nor teachers, nor bedrooms, nor birthdays, nor holidays, nor friends, etc. What I do remember is often sketchy. I do remember bathing and every time making sure the washcloth was over the keyhole. I remember a life full of fear. A life where I constantly looked for trees to climb—to hide in. I remember longing to be ugly and beautiful and simultaneously. I remember being baptized in Texas and my first day in Germany being raped under the pretext of showing me the apartment the whole family was to be moved into—I was allegedly supposed to be making sure that it was ready for everyone. Just before the bastard left for Thailand, he came back up the stairs so he could 'steal' a French kiss one last time before I was safe. Yeh, 'safe' with Gary.

Leslie, you might consider the fact that while you may CONSIDER your life to be bitter, mine WAS a living hell.

I never like hearing from any human being that their lives have been 'bitter.' It is a sad thing to hear and an even sadder thing to have to witness. I have heard and witnessed it from both of you. So, I hope you will both understand that I do not intend to perceive my life as 'bitter.' For me, what is left is very precious. I believe that both of you will readily understand that I might choose to expend my time and energies with those who treat me with dignity and respect.

If there are lists to be made, I suggest that the two of you make them for and about each other. I do have problems remembering a time in the last 15 or so years when I have been alone with one of you and you have not been complaining about the other.

When the child is not heard because children seldom have a voice which is listened to; when the child becomes an adult and is then told that they are to forgive and forget, that this all happened in the past; is this not the same as telling this human being that what has occurred is of no consequence?

As a child, I kept silent because I believed my world would end because the adults around me told me it was so. I was never told, 'I'll kill you.' No, I was told that 'it' would kill your mother and/or he would kill my brother. Later, I am told to be concerned with killing Grandmother as well. The adults told me they loved me and, as a child does, I believed them. They were my world. My world was those adults, those adults who might die. So concerned was I for them, where is their concern for me? Here's another assignment—put together your lists of what I have done. I don't fear your lists. If I could really remember, would either of you fear mine? You see the memory is almost totally blank before age 8. I may never know whether that means a damn thing or not. You see, when adults mess with little kids, they can really do a number on them.

L

P.S. Leslie, your letter arrived a bit late as the zip code was wrong."

A copy was mailed to Leslie and to Grandmother. And now, here come the bombs....

Chapter 6
The Bombs

Postmarked 8 Sept 93, the first reply was from Lynnette:

"Dear Lyn:

Your duplicate letters came yesterday. I am very hurt. For from the moment of your birth I have loved you and one of the things that has helped me has been my belief that you really cared for me. I look all around me and see all the different gifts you have given me. I had thought with love. I had no idea that you really hate me but it is now burned into my mind.

I am not going to go into any discussion with you. For one thing a verbal discussion would lead to a quarrel and I refuse to have one with you or anyone else. For another thing it would probably lead to me either having another trip to the hospital or my death. Now my funeral is all paid for and taken care of but I cannot afford another time in the hospital. And I am not positive it would mean my death.

GG"

I decide, at this time, I am not going to directly respond to this tirade. I am not certain why she requested the lists originally, but apparently there is to be no discussion which apparently would lead to a quarrel and the possibility of her demise. I'm pretty disgusted by the entire letter.

I did at one point toy with the idea of making that good/bad list set and the memory problems that have been addressed elsewhere in this writing, truly interfered. What I could remember that might have been thought of as positive, had the markings of Leslie's face all over them. What I mean by this is what was given was not given to me but to appearance.

Thou shalt not shame her in public.

Thou shalt not bring down the scorn of those outside the family unit.

Thou shalt not damage her façade.

As if to lend credence this theory, about a little over a week later, Leslie's bomb hit the mailbox:

"14 Sept 1993

Dearest Lynnette,

I have loved you ever since you were put into my arms after you were born. And I shall love you always.

You are always welcome anytime you care to come here.

Please do not add to your pain by feeling that my life has been bitter. It has only had bitter episodes for I have many beautiful memories of the past and hope to have many more before the Lord calls me to leave this world.

I have many friends who love me and I enjoy being with them and 2 children, 8 grandchildren and 9 great Grandchildren I love.

I pray that you will find peace and relief from your pain of many years.

Love Mom"

Who the hell cued the violin section? The following was sent in reply to Leslie, almost a month later:

"18 Sept 93

'I pray that you will find peace and relief from your pain of many years.' The Deity is neither responsible for my pain, nor for my relief from it. It is my responsibility, as it is a Deity-given responsibility for <u>all of us</u>. I don't know what is worse, the patronizing, the whining, or the venom. If it makes the two of you feel better to presume me ungrateful and/or mentally unstable, it is certainly within your realm of rights to do so. If that is the case, please do keep residing in your personally prescribed gingerbread houses. However, it would be appreciated if you'd both keep your ego-defensive crap to yourselves. I've been dumped on enough in my childhood to know when attempts are being made to dump on me again. I pray the two of you are granted greater understandings/knowledge of yourselves. This will naturally lead to an increase in your respective compassion levels, when it is combined with the love you two have always alleged to have held for me. I pray this occurs soon, as it seems to me that I have been attempting to draw from two very dry wells.

Lyn"

A week later, the 25th at approximately 7:15 p.m., I receive a phone call from Grandmother. My notes read:

I don't know what I did to be hated this way.

I don't hate you. You assumed from the letter that I had accused you—that pissed me off.

Something to the effect that: I don't know why you hate me. You've hastened my death. I've been very ill….

Interrupting her I said, I don't need this, and I hung up.

If someone had told me that I would be hanging up on my grandmother, I would not have been able to conceive of the possibility prior to this event. That night I wrote to her as follows:

"9/25/93

I received this letter from you approximately two weeks ago (copy attached). Now, I get this phone call....

Why <u>YOU</u> have decided to believe that I hate, I don't know. Why <u>YOU</u> seem to think it's okay to keep threatening me with your life, I don't know either.

I do know that your death and any trips to the hospital are strictly between you and your God.

Between Leslie's pious prattle and your attempts at guilt trips/manipulation I have just about had it with both of you. Why on earth do either of you choose to behave like this?"

Silence. It is not until about two months later that I am subjected to communications again. Oh yes, let us now have the weapons of Christmas brought into the fray.

Chapter 7
The War On Christmas

The first holiday card is received on the 27th of November.

"May you have the spirit of Christmas which is peace... The gladness of Christmas which is hope...The heart of Christmas which is love." So reads the greeting card. She also writes: Let there be Peace between us, And let it begin with me.

With Love GG"

The following reply was written on the 30th, <u>but not mailed</u>:

"'Peace' is a word and evoking it does not automatically produce what the word symbolizes. What has changed?

Has it occurred to you that it is not okay to attempt to browbeat someone into submission; using as a club the very love you have so indignantly proclaimed I do not hold for you? Has it occurred to you that by threatening me with your life you have attempted to trample on my love of you—using my love as a weapon against me? Sam did that. Does it suddenly become 'alright' because it is you who attempts the abuse?

That I love you is extremely evident in the pain I feel, but I refuse any longer to take on the pain/guilt for something which is/was done to me."

21 December brings one package which arrives United Parcel and one package via the U.S. mail. Both are from Figi's. Presents

from Leslie, that are both returned on the 23rd. Unopened and with no explanation.

The 24th U.S. Priority mail brings a present from Grandmother. There is a different Christmas card inside but she's written: "My love for you is eternal." That card and the present, were returned on the 27th.

These attempts of manipulation are beneath the conversation I sought to have. I'm pretty disgusted. If all you wish to offer me is to threaten your demise, bribery with gifts, and the quotation of pious words, I think you need to rethink our relationship.

The lesson learned when Doris landed in Germany was: If the door to hell is not closed, the devil returns. This is the path of passive aggression as well as the path of the physical abuser. Returning to the fold now would certainly find me taking little smacks to the ass as I pass.[34] And at this point would find me the target of barbs due to the pain caused by open wounds they carry because they will not allow the conversations necessary for all of us to heal. I can't do it for them. They can't do it for me. Our relationships are broken. What are these relationships based on?

The laying of "gifts" is not the laying of hands. The laying of gifts is bribery. Laying gifts is the showmanship of the tithing in public. The laying of gifts is how you placate a god that you seek favor from. (Oh yeah, the devil made me do it, let me give you a hug.)

---

[34] Note: This actually had happened almost 2 years prior. The more I pressed Leslie about the length of time it took her to get divorced, the more apparent the passive/aggression was becoming— even to the point of smacking me as I passed her. Mind you, I am in my 40's when she does this. All you had to do is see her facial expression when she did this to know it was not...playful?

The laying of hands is the outreach of love with the intent to heal, to meet with another halfway with compassion born of our own self-knowledge. The laying of hands is an acknowledgment of our bond with the universe, the bond we have as a part of humanity.

Apparently, I am to be cajoled. No amount of sweet talking is going to bar me from the path I am on. As I mentioned in one of the earlier letters—if you won't protect me, I will.

There was no communication until April of 1994, four months later.

Chapter 8
1994, The Uninvited Guest

I received a short note from Grandmother that is dated April 1994:

"Dearest Lyn and Jay: Regardless of how much you hate me, I still love you as I have all of your life. I realize you will probably will send this back unread but I had to at least make the effort to reach you. With Love your Grandmother."

What is interesting is that for the first time, the letter and its contents are addressed to my husband as well. Addressing Jay again is the next note which was received on the 28th of May:

"Dear Lyn and Jay: Although you feel that you do not want to be a part of this family, we still love both of you and I am writing to tell you that Mary Catherine, your Uncle Tom's wife passed away May 1st and was buried two days later.

We hope all is going well with you since you have cut yourself from the family and that you have accomplished whatever you were searching for.

I really do love you and will forever.

Your Grandmother,

Lynnette"

I had received a call from my daughter the night before. She told me that she had gotten a letter from GG that told of Mary Kate's death. She was also concerned because GG had not mentioned anything about her going into the Air Force and that it was odd because she had mentioned it in her last letter.

She then called GG and they spoke of Mary Kate and the Air Force and then GG began on how horrible I was. My daughter told her of my being fired and her response was to the effect that she wasn't surprised considering the frame of mind I'd been in lately. Basically, according to what my daughter was told, I am rude and off-the-deep-end.

My daughter's concern stems from the deviation from the norm in Grandmother's behavior. Normally Grandmother would be attentive about her upcoming challenge. Normally Grandmother would be very supportive. Luckily, I had already spoken to my daughter concerning what was happening.

I had specifically stated to her that this was between the 3L's— Leslie, Lynnette, and Lyn. The older generations had some work to do and, as far as I was concerned, there was no problem with her maintaining her relationships with them. I had told her to expect that there would be anger directed at me, and that perhaps her best response would be to state that "that" is between you and my mother.

Since the beginning of my life, I have always played the role of liaison between my mother and grandmother. As I mentioned in one of the previous letters, often either my grandmother or my mother would complain to me about the other. It's a very strange tightrope to walk. I was concerned that Grandmother was trying to bring my daughter into that role. As it turned out, there was no reason for me to be concerned. Between her up-coming basic training with the Air

Force and Grandmother's deteriorating mental state, this would not happen.

Unknown to me at the time, Grandmother was going downhill mentally. This is mentioned in the next letter I received from Leslie. Unfortunately, I am wounded to the point of not being able to believe a word that comes from either of these icons in my life. I am not certain what Leslie's reasoning was for informing me of Lynnette's condition. Whatever it was, I did not respond.

My response was the one thing Leslie was looking for. Again, the situation had not changed. I had nothing to work with except the potential for servitude.

"23 June 1994

Lynnette—

Just a short note I hope you will read. I can understand what has happened between us but I cannot understand why you are unhappy with G.G. She has always cared what happened to you.

I don't know what she said to you after I told her but I am sure it was brought about because in her generation you denied these things happened.

She will be 90 in Aug. and is able to get about and take care of herself at present.

In the month of Jan, she was very ill and I took care of her here. It was a problem with her lungs. She is not remembering things at times and becomes a little confused.

Please, I hope you find it your heart to contact her.

If I can help you at any time please remember where I am.

Love

Mom"

Lynnette has said many things but not once has she denied what happened to me. The generational argument is interesting but not valid. Finally, after digesting these last few communiqués, I sit down and write the following letter which I do not mail:

"2 July 1994

The last communication I received from Lynnette attempted to berate me for not attending a funeral that had occurred three weeks earlier. Threatening me with her early demise is one thing, but utilizing the death of another is extremely distasteful. While you have repeatedly chosen to accept (thus reinforce) such chicken shit behavior, I will not.

Your letter asks that I re-enter a situation that I know to be abusive. Sam stated he loved and cared for me, and just like you and Lynnette, I'm quite sure he believed it too.

Tell me, what have I done to warrant such treatment? I was raped for close to a decade of my life; I finally gain enough fortitude to ask why the two most important women in my life did not remove me from harm's way and what is the result? BOTH react with guilt. Unadmitted guilt attacks what it feels guilty about. (You experienced these dynamics enough times with Sam to be an expert!)

Don't ask ME what you're both reacting to—ask yourselves. The worst of it is that the two of you have now really left me wondering about what I don't remember.

I don't suppose it might have occurred to either of you that there might be times I need protection. But then neither of you can give me what you do not have the moral courage to give yourselves.

I'm glad you can understand what has happened between us---all I can see is waste."

The next letter I get from Grandmother is addressed to me alone. I guess she's determined my husband is not interested in entering our communiques.

Postdated 21 July 1994:

"Dear Lyn:

Although I realize that you, only thinking of yourself, do not realize how you can hurt other people especially someone like me. I have loved you from your first breath and your grandpa did also. Your birth caused us to give up the life we had planned for we two together but because of the love we had for you and your mother we set aside the plans we had made. Not once but three times, first when you were born, second when Mac was born and the third time when you, Mac and your mother came from Kentucky, just before your grandpa died.

We all make mistakes. Mine has been that I love my children and grandchildren so much that I have always tried to help them and have done it their way.

Forgiveness is really a beautiful thing. Because I have forgiven my own children of the things, I have had happen to me because of them I can look forward to more peaceful life.

Please put aside your hatred.

No matter how you decide this will be the last time I shall write you unless you request it.

I do love you. GG"

If she has "forgiven," it doesn't sound like it from this letter. A month later I received a birthday card the day before my birthday. So much for not writing me unless I request it.

"To my most loved, first grandchild

'May this Birthday wish keep adding to every day—all year a little something extra in the way of joy—and cheer!'

With Love

GG"

I'm still digesting the last communique from Lynnette when Leslie shows up at my door. Now begins my Birthday from Hell! <u>The pre-printed, commercial message on the card she hands me reads:</u>

"'Dear Daughter,

I'm proud of the way you've grown up. I admit I still worry at times because the world has changed a lot since you were born. Many of the choices you've had to make have been more difficult than those I faced when I was your age. I haven't always agreed with your decisions, but I hope you know that I respect your courage and independence in making them. You're doing all you can to be the person you want to be, and I admire that...And remember—no matter what life brings, you will always be my daughter, and I will always love you. Happy Birthday'

Mom"

She shows up at the door at 6:45 p.m. Brings card. I'm told she has Parkinson's and GG is deteriorating. Tom (her brother) won't talk to Grandmother, and Thank God! Mac has been there the whole year.

She doesn't remember that her Granddaughter, went into the Air Force today. I kicked her out of my home. Her parting words were: "I had to wait until I was 69 to find out I was a lousy mother."

145

Those were the last words my ears would hear from her, and the last time I would physically see her. There would be additional letters before she died on Thanksgiving 2000. Six years later.

The two birthday cards carried the "right "words but actions speak much louder than words. Grandmother knew when she sent her card that Leslie was descending on me. After having told me that she would not force herself on me, she forced herself on me.

Chapter 9
The Remainder Of 1994

The Birthday from Hell was over and all is quiet for about two months. Then on October 15th, I receive correspondence from Grandmother again. This time it takes the form of a letter I had sent her about 6 months prior to my "TRUTH" letter of August 1993.

"15 February 1993

Dear Grandmother—

Egads! I've gotten two letters within a period of 7 days. That typewriter of yours must still be smokin'.

We all had a rather pleasant surprise about a week ago. Sean wrote Cathy & Tim and apologized AND paid them back in full all the money he owed them. I'm glad it has worked out this way for everyone concerned. I know it was really tearing at Cathy for a while there.

I'm having problems with Willie Nelson being given a deal with his taxes too. Sometimes I feel that our entire society is set up to simply 'take' anyone who 'obeys' its rules. It's like do what I say so I can take you to the cleaners faster. However, I then get to thinking about how one would have to live and feel trying to hide and I remember why I pay when I'm supposed to. It can sure make you crazy though if you let it....

Oh, have I got a recipe for you!! Jay's been making it for about three weeks now. You take a package of mucacholli (my spelling on this is terrible and the dictionary I have doesn't have the word!!!!) and cook it up according to directions. In a large skillet you take 2 tblsp crushed garlic, 3/4th stick of butter, about 3 tblsp olive oil, about a ½ lbs thick sliced fresh mushrooms, and chopped green onions and sauté until the mushrooms and onions are just UNDER-done. Now add the macaroni, mix, and then add about 8oz of freshly grated parmesan cheese—mix though and dig in. It is wonderful!!!!

I am glad you care for Moonshine; it makes me feel good to know that you, of all people, have a doll that I made.

The weather has been such a bear of late. It's snowing slightly even as I type this to you. I'm SOOOOOOOOOO ready for spring!

Cathy bought me some earrings from her store. They are really pretty. Slightly heavy silver hoops with a stone which changes colors as I move my head. I've worn them almost constantly since she gave them to me about a week ago.

I want to make sure this gets into the mailbox. Take care. I love you.

Love as always,

Lynnette'

At the base of the letter, she has handwritten:

Lyn: Did you really write this? I believed you then. GG"

This writing of mine is an excellent example of the level of communication that she and I developed over the years. It is meant as something of a slap in the face by her, and it does its job well because I do miss the level of friendship we had.

"Moonshine," the doll…. I had made Moonshine because I had heard that Grandmother was having health problems. I had understood that those problems seemed to worsen around the full moon. The doll's dress had been made from a blouse I had that I had dearly loved and worn past its usefulness. It was something of a bright, jungle print—mostly blues and greens. There was ample, useable material to make the dress for the doll. Moonshine also had a fairly good-sized Moonstone attached to her collar. Grandmother was always making dolls, so I used that as an excuse to get the Moonstone close to her as she slept. The doll, for a time, was on her bed.

About a month later, the next letter arrives and the knives are definitely out:

"Monday November 21, 1994

My dearest and first grandchild:

Even while writing this, I do not know if you are still hating me. And if you are it is a sad return for the love, I have always had for you.

And as for your nastiness concerning your mother—I can remember several times when you could have told me what was going on. Times when we were alone and if told me what was going on, I could have stopped it. For instance, when I visited you in Germany. At that time, I had the power to have put a stop to what was going on. Oh, no I am not just writing foolishly. I belonged to a family with connections in Washington, DC and also with the military. A whisper in the right ear was all that was needed. But all of those connections are now gone and I can do nothing.

Do you know what fear is? The dictionary says (among other meanings) fear is a continuing state or attitude of fright, dread or terror as in to live in fear. In spite of the fear Leslie had of her husband she went to the officers of his battalion or whatever they call his group and to the Chaplain and as most do, they said there was nothing they could do against him. They wanted nothing like that to come out in their command. I have talked to some of my military friends who now or have been up again just the same thing. And they say it is often that way.

I am now in my 90s, and for some reason I am still living. But for what reason? I have given the best of my life to you and to Leslie and now I look back on the sacrifices that I made for you and wonder if any of it was worth it. Now I feel that nothing I have done was worth it. Now I feel that nothing I have done was worthwhile. And yet somehow, I still love both of you.

GG

Sacrifices you wonder.

First Leslie comes home to have you, then she goes to work and we have your care. So, we missed the trips and things we had planned.

Then when she divorced Jim, she brought you home again. We cared for you again what we had planned forgotten. Then down in Texas—Oh I wasn't expected to have a life of my own.

Then again you came to Leavenworth and for love I cared for your children. No, I did not exist except to wait on children, and all because I loved all of you and really thought I was doing something good for all of you. Now I know it was just a waste of my time."

I would learn latter that the family power connections were very real. The problem with knowledge is that you have to know it exists in order to utilize it. I certainly didn't know at age sixteen, but Leslie did. If Leslie knew, it's quite possible that Sam did too.

My reply, which took six days to get down on paper, was <u>never sent</u>:

"27 November 1994

It would seem you have been given the Leslie digested condensed version of what occurred up here in August. But hey, that is definitely not surprising!

Do you have any awareness as to how pathetic these "lovely," little notes of yours are? "…as for your nastiness concerning you Mother…." "Nastiness?" Loathe!! Before the slime ball left, she had informed me that you and I have always sought to control her and that you had not raised her but her father and her Grandparents did. I believe she was attempting to make a last-ditch effort to say to me that this was why she herself was such a lousy Mother.

But I am sure that such statements from her would not surprise you as they come from Leslie's "Twisted mind" and are a result of her being some type of McBratney genetic defect (as you have put in writing). As I told Leslie, when she descended upon me without an invitation, you are both 2-faced, backstabbing whores. I do regret the "whore" part, but only because it would be far more accurate to describe the both of you as "pimps." (You two don't have the honor code of whores.)

Oh yes, do inform Leslie that the next time she attempts to make a PHYSICALLY AGGRESSIVE maneuver I will forget about how long it might take to explain to a Judge how I came to deck a 70-year-old woman! When I straight-armed her, it was like landing into a mess of cotton candy. Get a grip on reality, Les! I honestly believe the bitch thought I feared her. She sits there and takes 2-days' worth of verbal abuse—it took THAT LONG to get it through her skull that I don't give a shit folks!!! Least I forget---Les, I caught you reading Lynnette's birthday card to me. I caught you at it long enough to catch the look on your face. Also, the next time you give someone a birthday cared it is customary to sign it. Thanks, loads you two, it was a simply marvelous way to spend my birthday. You both seem to have an extraordinary talent for pissing me off.

Tell me, Madam, why should your Granddaughter feel safe confiding in you when your own Daughter didn't until this Granddaughter finally did!! Judging from the results, I think that even if I had told you, at the time, I would have regretted it. Besides, why should I NEED to inform you, Oh High & Mighty Woman of Someone Else's Power, when I had already told: 1. A woman neighbor in Burkburnett (which eventually led to having Sam investigated by the Air Force); 2. When I had told LESLIE TWICE (The first time she was told was when the Ramstein AFB police questioned Sam. He came home, grabbed me by the hair, and yanked/pulled me up the stairs finally, throwing me at the foot of the bed in which Leslie was sleeping—he then demanded that I tell her what I HAD DONE! (The 3rd time Gary was told and she HAD to act.) (So much for your Daughter-in-fear-acting-in-

courage routine!; 3. When I had told the man I loved, Gary; and 4. When I had told a Minister—supposedly of God! Hell Honey, everyone in the world was told but you!!! (Think about it!) As for this 16-year-old-I-am-not-legally-an-adult-person-as-of-yet.... The ONLY thing which held Sam in check was KNOWING that Gary would do whatever was necessary. Sam already KNEW, from experience, that Leslie wouldn't do a damn thing. You see, I have this major problem with lovely Leslie.... On the one hand she says that I decided not to press charges; that I decided not to go and live with you— and yet, she does not mention MY DESIRING to get married and to MOVE-OUT. I was TOLD, as this 16-year-old-I-am-not-legally-an-adult-person-as-of-yet, that no way do I even get an engagement ring until I have my high school diploma. (There is something humorous in not being allowed an engagement ring when you haven't been a virgin in over a decade.) Nor does Leslie mention or seem to be aware of the men Sam kept throwing at me trying to get me to break off with Gary. On the one hand, Leslie keeps telling me what a lousy Mother you were and yet Mac & I keep getting dropped in your lap. No matter which one of you two are telling the truth on this one, she loses because what a caring, devoted, courageous Mother she must be to drop her kids off with someone she has repeatedly stated she has experienced as being an inadequate/neglectful Mother.

Now, while I am on the topic of people saying one thing & then doing another.... "Sacrifices you wonder." Sacrifices indeed!! Vaguely I remember a mythological figure called GG. This wondrous being was cloaked with integrity and honor. I can distinctly remember her telling me something over and over and over again, over the years. I remember her telling me something that I thought was so right and beautiful, that I adopted it as part of my own actions. She said, "Whatever I give I always give with no strings attached." I don't regret all the letters, all the conversations, all the things I have freely done for you. Nor do I regret the seemingly brief period in my life where I was able to honor and respect the woman, who I at one time called, Mother. But I deeply resent being infringed upon now.

These letters of yours serve only to remind me of why I've closed the door on both of you. I don't have the time for the bitterness and hatred the two of you exhibit in person and in your writings. You have both repeatedly made it abundantly clear that you would rather try to beat me down than look into your own hearts. I find it very unfortunate that both of you continue to believe that you must live together hating each other the whole while. No, I guess I don't know what I am talking about.... But I DO KNOW WHAT THE TWO OF YOU HAVE TOLD ME ABOUT EACH OTHER OVER THE YEARS, INCLUDING 1994. The truth is that this sick and twisted relationship that the two of you have, left the door open for Sam to enter. Even now you allow him to scar me—even now you allow him to separate me from those who are supposed to protect me—even now you two would rather blame the victim than face up to what you two have done and continue to do to each other. I'll not be a part of such sickness.

Don't talk to me of sacrifice, Lynnette! Don't talk to me about what love and caring have cost you. I who have no father, no mother, no grandmother, no brother. THE FAMILY the two of you have so fictitiously created over the years I gladly leave. As you stated in your last (I can only Hope!) letter: "Now I know it was just a waste of my time." Whatever loyalty existed vanished, evaporated when you told me that all the love and caring that I had experienced at your hand had a price tag and that the price of your love is blind devotion. You told me to look up the word "fear." I say to you, "Look up the word, 'slavery'." Just as the slaves took new names, I am no longer known as Lynnette. Or is that something else that Leslie failed to mention!"

Even now I am grateful that I determined that this reply of mine did not reach the postal system. These unsent missives of mine, while therapeutic at the time they are written, they remain difficult to absorb. I am so very angry. I am so very hurt. So are they.

In December I receive two Christmas cards from my Grandmother. The first one, received on the 15th, is simply signed

"With Love GG." The 2nd card which was received on the 20th: *"Can you not forgive—hatred is like a poison eating away not only those you hate but those who really love you—I still do even though you hate me. Your Grandmother"*

At this point, I am determined not to reply to any attempts at correspondence. We even have an answering machine now and do not pick up unless we wish too. I have decided to leave them with their fantasy. It is obvious at this point that I can't evoke change, and I don't want to play the game they are in….

Chapter 10
1995, The Year I Stop Communicating

February 16, 1995 is what the postmark reads.

"Dear Lyn:

Regardless of what you think of what you have done or what you think I have done, Why do you not realize that I sincerely love you and miss you very much.

Don't you think it is about time for you to begin to realize that I am part of your life and that someday you will realize how badly I have been hurt by you and you will wish you had made your peace with me.

You have always been nearest and closest of my grandchildren.

Please give this some thought for I do really love you.

GG"

March 22 is the postmark on the next letter. This one is from Leslie.

"Lynnette—

Please read this as I think it is information you need to know.

Feb 23rd your Grandmother spent the day in bed which is not like her.

At 3am that night I heard her knock the soap dish in the bathroom then until 5 am she started passing out—became very weak. And I call 911 took her to hospital she was in shock.

It was decided that she had anemia, dehydration and was bleeding rectally. She also was bruised all over.

She was admitted to the hospital after a sigmoidoscopy(?) & Ba Exxx(?) it was decided she did not have cancer.

The final diagnosis was that the bruising and bleeding was due to accumulation of her blood thinner in her body.

She stayed 5 days and is home now still able to go to the bathroom and bath and dress herself but is very weak and easily tired. She spends most of her days in bed or on the couch. Reading or watching T.V. Only place she goes is to have her hair done and I took her in the car. Mom"

The next letter to arrive is dated four days after Leslie's:

"March 26, 1995

Dear Lyn and Jay: Tomorrow I shall write and have witnessed my last will and testament. I am doing this because of the things that have happened to me in the past two years. I no longer believe that anyone in my family cares one bit about me. But I have always promised to you for instance, the walnut bed dresser and mattress etc. I will leave them to you, legally so you can dispose of them in any matter you wish, even junk them.

I am now 90 years and 8 months old and have returned from my third serious visit to the hospital. My time on earth is about done and while I will not speed the time, I have left neither shall I try to stay.

Even though you doubt it I still love you. GG"

Two and a half months later another letter from Lynnette arrives:

"Sunday, June 11, 1995

Dear Lyn and Jay:

I am writing you because of two things. First, I have always promised Lyn the walnut bedroom furniture and I must know whether she still wants it and if you two will be able to come and get it. Soon. If I do not hear from you concerning it say within a month, I will consider that you do not want it.

The next thing I feel that I should let you know that Leslie came thru her operation very well and is, while somewhat weak almost back or even better health.

And so, I remain although I know you hate me

Your loving GG"

Then, in about three months I receive the following:

"10 October 1995

Dear Lyn and Jay:

My typewriter is being fixed so this scrawl will have to do.

Yes, I am still alive although 91 years old. I do not know if you will answer this or not because you have allowed yourself to fill up with hate but; I have always loved you, Lyn. All of your life. I have done everything I could to make your life better. I do hope that before I die I will see you again.

All around me are reminders that I thought were given me in love. I had always felt that you really cared for me. I would like to come to Omaha and see you one more time. Don't worry I would <u>not</u> come to your home but would go to motel. Leslie would have to bring me but you do not need to see her.

I also need to know if you want the oak bedroom set when I am gone—or before I go if you want it.

If I do not receive an answer, I will know you are still full of hate

But I do love you as I always have

Grandmother

Jay you are on my Love List—very near the top."

The envelope was dated December 11th.

"Dear Lyn and Jay:

This is the last time you will ever hear from me unless there is an answer from you.

It is very hard for me who am I love very much should be so full of hate that you have hurt me thru and thru.

I do not know if you want the bedroom set that I promised you. If I do not hear and very soon it will no longer be yours. You can either come and get it yourselves, or send someone to pick it up.

My time is growing short so I may not be here and even if I were still alive, I will plan to be absent.

For you to turn from Love to hate, you would not be someone I would want to see.

Strangely I still love you

GG"

Christmas card postdated 18 December:

"Why am I being punished for what I did not do? I always tried to do all I could for my beloved ones and now that I can almost count the time on Earth that I may live I am getting hatred instead of Love. I still Love you very much—GG"

Chapter 11
1995, My Year Of Learning

"8 Jan 1996

Dear Lynnette,

Please read this regardless of how you feel about me.

Your GRANDMOTHER is now 91 years old. She is not critically ill at present but is holding every hurt she has had in her life and one of those the loss of contact with her oldest Granddaughter.

Please do not <let?> your feelings about me keep you from contact with you. She has loved you very dearly all of your life and anything she may have said when you terminated our relationship was only because she was shocked and defending her daughter as you would defend Cathy.

If you wish at any time wish to make contact with her it can be arranged for me to be out of your way.

If you ever need or want me in any I am here.

Hoping you will find it in your heart to fulfill one of your Grandmothers desires I close.

MOM"

I am not writing to Lynnette for the same reasons I am not writing to Leslie and one of those reasons is definitely not because her mother is defending her daughter.

Envelope was postdated 22 Jan 96:

"Dear Lyn and Jay:

Starting with you these are probably be the last letters I will write to my Grandchildren. I love each of them very much. Your Grandpa and I had planned that when he was retired and with all three of our children now adults, we would sell the house and build one down on the Ozark Lake. We even had the place picked out where he could fish and enjoy life. But our children still needed us. Your Grandpa was fatefully ill and he was home for a short time when your Mother, you and Sean came home. When she decided to marry again, I sold the house and went to a college so that I could have a career. I don't know what was intended for me but exactly after my graduation, and just when I was trying to decide which of two promising jobs to take your Uncle Jack called me from Des Moines. It seems he was called to put in a month with the Navy Reserves and as Bunnie could not manage alone could I come and stay with his family. Oh, another need was that Bunnie was expecting. So, I cancelled my interviews and off to Des Moines. Jack's Navy time had been set back a month but it was lucky that I was there. He was at a Navy meeting and the weather is or rather was like today…so much snow we can't see a block and the wind howling. Well Jack home got her to the hospital and she had a ceasar…I guess that is the way to spell it. Anyway, it was a girl and when was named Bridget. I stayed until Bunnie was back on her feet and then went to Kansas City to see Tom's. And from there I went to Waco, the weatherman was sent to Alaska and I stayed to care for you two as your Mother had to work to care for you. Then he returned and I left to go to Jack's where they needed me for, they had moved to California and they were having another and last child, Teresa. What caused me to give up any life of my own? It was the love I have for my grandchildren. My adult children could care for themselves but my grandchildren were more precious than anything else. I am trying to write all ten of you to remind you that I tried to make life better for all of you.

Now I am old and frail. I am 91 and I hope you will sometime remember that I loved you dearly. You will not be bothered by another letter.

May the rest of your life be good for you.

With LOVE GG"

There's a lot of family information that I did not know in this letter. It is easy to see that she made many decisions based on Leslie remarrying and Jack's call to aid his wife. These decisions placed her on a path that she continued as her children kept requesting that she come and help them. Never the less, these are her decisions.

There are some hard lessons in life that I learned from Lynnette. You cannot choose to give and then expect payment in kind. It won't happen. It will seem to happen right up to the moment it is determined you are no longer required. It will seem to happen right up to the moment you begin to believe that you might have a voice in the decisions that are being made.

If you believe that you are going to have a voice in the decisions that are being made and you attempt to use that voice, that vote, you will quickly learn your true position. This happens time and time again with each of her three adult children and later, with some of her grandchildren.

It is not wrong to ask for help. It is not wrong to give aid. This is a transaction and it is either given freely with no thought of gain, or it is contracted up front with all parties involved.

I've seen this "non-contract" assistance a lot when it comes to women. Not so much with men, which is not to say that I have not witnessed this with men. My present husband is one example of giving without expectation, especially in regard to his parents. I have seen this and I honor it for what it is, but it was not done for me or anyone else to honor the actions.

Anyone acting to aid another selflessly does not resent the aiding of another. The gift given by the giver is the acknowledgement that they have something of value to give. That is payment enough if you are doing this simply because you can because you decide to.

Received about three months later and postmarked 5 April 1996:

"Dear Lyn and Jay:

Although it has been a long time since you let me know that you did not care for me to write to you, and as I am almost 92 and near my time on earth, I wanted one more time to let you know that ever since your birth I have loved you dearly.

Your Grandmother Lynnette McBratney"

Another letter arrives a month later:

"May 6, 1996

Dear Lyn,

This is the last time you will hear from you unless you either write me and say you would like to see me. It has been very hard for me not to at least hear from you. It is difficult for me and has hurt me very much to have you out of my life. From the moment you were born you have been, except for the Love I had and cherished from your Grandpa and since 1957 when he died you have been my dearest love.

What happened between your Mother and you should not have affected what I thought you felt for me. But all this has ruined my feelings for her. I still live with her as she always has, she needs me. And so, I have to feel that you do not care for me.

Strangely I still care for you,

Your Grandmother GG"

The window has finally opened for me to crawl through as she acknowledges that "What happened between your Mother and you should not have affected what I thought you felt for me." The next few lines give me pause. I really do not want to get into the Leslie vs Lynnette, apparently on-going, battle again.

To this letter, I did reply. The reply was handwritten on the original letter she sent after I copied it word for word:

"I love you. I understand. I do care. But, let's go slow. Things are not the same as they were. Leslie is not to be discussed. Nor is Mac. I have no Brother. I've never had a Father. I'd like to hang onto my Grandmother, but I'd really like to communicate with my life-long Friend, Lynnette.

For the record.... February 3, 1996 Ashton Lynnette-Marie. GGG?

Strangely I still care for you too,

Lyn"

Chapter 12
The Flood Gates Open

As I render this, I regret not having saved my letters to her during this time period. The back and forth of our communications were always so…back and forth.

As I received these letters from her, so filled with the comings and goings of family, I was somewhat overwhelmed. Mentioned in the letter that follows, "A Mealman Family Genealogy," was sent to me by Lynnette. The 176-page self-published, hardbound book was produced and copyrighted by D.R. Mealman in 1996. I have now gone from knowing practically nothing of family to knowing a line from prior to the American Revolution, replete with stories and pictures and documentation.

May 14, 1996

My dearest Lyn—I am so delighted to receive your letter. Both conditions agreed to. Just so I hear from you. Is the baby Sean's?

Everything is in such a mess as I am trying to have this go easy for those I leave behind. For I am due to not last much longer. Anyway, if I do what has been requested of me—I will live to be 100.

First, I must tell you that I hope that I shall have a genealogy of my Mother's family stemming from the French and Indian Wars to today. If I can get enough copies and if you would like to have one, I will send you one.

Whose baby is it that you sent? I have not heard from Cathy. I heard from someone that Sean's wife was expecting the baby, boy or girl is darling.

I have had three heart attacks—very seldom leave the house except to have medicine refilled but am doing well for an almost 93.

About the baby—if I am a GGG (Great, great, great grandmother—Please remember I adore GG-GGG or whatever.

Please give my Love to Jay—I guess he is still around.

Carolyn said to give you her Love—she is very busy helping Arthur and Ruth. Both are on walkers. Arthur both hips broken by falls, at separate times. He is retired and Ruth has fallen so many times. Mary Catherine died about a year ago.

Do you still want the bed and dresser? I do love you very much.

G"

This is the first time I am hearing about her three heart attacks. It appears that my husband may be on her naughty list? She seems a bit confused as to which of her great-grandchildren has become a parent. The newborn is a girl. It's good to know that Carolyn is still seeing her on what sounds like a regular basis.

Two weeks later, 28 May 1996, she writes:

"Memorial Day

Dear Lyn and Jay: A huge black cloud is hanging over us and tornado warnings are out. Saturday, I went to the Cemetery at the Fort and placed a wreath on your Grandpa's grave. And checked to be sure that they are holding my space next to him so that we can be together again. And I remembered when you were quite small and we were taking care of you and how you loved the trains and we would take you a certain place at a certain time and you would call out to the train and when it was gone you would settle right away and go to sleep. He really adored you, as I do and did.

Are Cathy and Tim out of the service? And how is Tim now? I like him very much and I love Cathy. I loved taking Cathy and Sean to school thru the snow-covered streets. I had a pair of boots that made fish designs in the snow and Sean liked to follow my trail.

Someway I have lost your letter and the one with the baby picture. You said a little girl? I would like their address so I can send her one of my dolls. I am preparing what must be coming. My death. Don't worry I will welcome it. And I am clearing things such as the furniture and many things. I cleared out my antique desk and as I had always promised it to Debbie, and Kevin will take it to her. She lost her husband and her Mother a couple of year ago. Mary Catherine had been very ill, in and out of Hospitals for a couple of years. They do not know how her husband died. She is in charge of a museum and art center in her town and had gone to a meeting in New Orleans. When she came back, he did not meet her plane. And they did not find him for about three weeks. In his car in an old garage some distance from town. No money on him. No wounds. Nothing to indicate the cause of his death. No Children.

Now to tell you two things. As you know I have a hundred and five families listed. From both my Mothers and Dads family and all of their families. Also, that I belong to the DAR. About eight years ago a man and his wife came calling on me. They had been to Washington and from the files there they found that my Revolution Ancestor was Adam Mealman. He was retired and they decided they would search out their decendency. Well, I knew that the original Adam Mealman was born in London and came to American Colonies as a British Soldier to fight in the French and Indian Wars. Then when the Revolutionary War came along, he fought with the Colonists. He spent that very cold winter at Valley Forge. George Washington was there and Mad Anthony Wayne. After the War was over, he established himself in the Pennsylvanian Mountains. But he fought in the War of 1812. Well they researched out all they could about Adam Mealman. He was descended from one of the sons and we are descended from his only daughter Nancy Mealman who married David Mills.

They gathered all the information they could and then published a Genealogy. Would you like a copy? If so, I have one you could have.

And there is something else to tell you. Maybe I already have told you. Any here goes.

Carolyn who lives here in L'worth, her sister Connie (remember the boy in the gray suit who ushered at the wedding of his sister and he was so handsome. He was married about a year ago) Connie is his Mother and one of Connie's girls went to Lincoln County largely to check on the cemeteries. My Dad's Family were buried in Hammer Cemetery. His Father and Mother, the six children they lost mostly as children, the woman that Dad married. She is with her husband, Beverly Cemetery where My Mother's people are buried and Lincoln the town's cemetery where Mother, Dad and both Warren and Juanita who were twins are buried. Anyway, there was a pink calling card stuck on the headstones. A Mrs. V. Davis, her address and written on the cards. I should like to hear from any Stanleys. Well, when Connie and Carolyn came back, they brought the card to me and asked just who she might be. Well, I knew. Dad was one of 17 Children. He was their fifth child. One of his older (Not Dads but his

XXXXX

Here one of the neighbors came in so now its two days later. For one thing I found your letter, it had slipped under the typewriter. To answer it..first. If you will send me Sean's address, I could send the baby and her older sister a couple of my dolls. I am beginning to clear out many things, dolls included and I want them to all have good homes.

I have already passed on to Carolyn and she will pass it on to Arthur and Ruth. He was 95 in March and she was 93 in April, she is three months older than I. Carolyn's daughter was here last week. She, Elizabeth lives in Sacramento. She has gone home now. One of Connie's sons wanted to be a farmer. He was married with children. Connie and Sherman had bought his home farm just before his parents died.

This thing of being old is for the birds. Anyway their son, Zane..Sherman's Mother was a Zane related to Zane Grey..His Mother was a niece of Zane Grey's Mother. Anyway. His wife said if that was what to be he had to go to Manhattan and take a course of the financial aspects. And so, he learned how to make money by having early crops. And he grows asparagus and strawberries this time of the year. And people can come and pick them and then they pay less. Each year I have bought ten pounds and someone in the family has always harvested them for me. This time Carolyn's Elizabeth cut the asparagus for me and brought it as a surprise.

I have been doing a little writing. Carolyn has a son named John. He and his wife have been married several years and always wanted children but no go. They were thinking of adoption when they had a baby boy. When it came time to name him, they thought of naming him after his Father Richard. But John happened to check the phone book and there were pages and pages of Richards. So, they decided to name him Adam for our ancestor and Arthur for Carolyn's Dad. Carolyn was here and we were talking about him and how they decided came to name him that way. So, I decided to write for him just a story about his name and I drew a little red uniform and three-cornered uniform hat and another solider with a blue uniform and the three-corner hat. Carolyn was delighted and so was Arthur. I have suggested Arthur write the story of his life as he can only read, write and watch TV. Also, for Adam. Arthur has so many visitors. It is I think 23 steps from the public side walk and as both he and Ruth are using Walkers they seldom leave the house. Carolyn does not live with she has a home on Broadway. She is their chauffer when they have to go out.

I seldom leave the house. Last Saturday I did go get a wreathe and took it to the cemetery at the Fort.

Give my love to Jay, Cathy, Tim and lots of it to you, Lyn"

I have to believe that there must be a billion people in this universe of ours who have in some form or another uttered: "Thank God for Carolyn!" The woman is a total treasure and you will find her mentioned quite a few times during this memoir. The various stories told here are precious to me.

The envelope is postmarked 17 September 1996:

"Tuesday

Dear Lyn and Jay: Thank you for sending Sean's address. And I hope that you had a good big laugh at my error. The older I get the dumber. And now please send me Cathy and Tim's. When in the service people do have a lot of moving to do.

I expect that the changing weather is having a bad effect on your spice plants. The garden of our neighbors has been affected. Ever since we moved in here, they have kept us supplied with stuff from their garden. They were about the only ones here who had nice tomatoes and now they...the tomatoes are gone.

I am sorry that Jay's Mother is not doing so well. I wish everyone getting older could be like me. Tho I am not able to do much, I watch so that I do not overdo. I dress, bathe, dress myself. Of course I am alone most of the time. I keep busy. I am right now making copies of letters that people long dead have written me concerning family stores.

Did I write you about the Lady with the pink calling card? Well, if I did here, I go again.

Carolyn and her sister went to Lincoln County to check on the three cemeteries where my Mother's people, my Dad's people and my Dad, Mother and their twins, Juanita and Warren are buried. It had always been my Dad and his family who had for almost a century to check and make sure all is well (One time my brother and my sisters decided that it was my turn. And they wanted peonies planted at each cemetery. If I remember the bulbs cost $75.00. And we had to hire a woman to see the bulbs were ready to plant and to plant them.

We went to Lincoln to see that all plots had peonies planted. Someone dug up and did steal all the bulbs.

So, Carolyn and Connie and a couple of Connie's girls to check at the cemetery they found stuck to the grave stones of the Stanley graves with scotch tape there was the pink calling card. On the cards were written Would like to contact any of the Stanleys. Well since I seem to be the one that messes around with families they brought the cards to me. I wrote her and she answered and answered and answered. It seems that Velma is the granddaughter of my Dad's sister who was named Sadie. My Dad with the fifth of seventeen. And she married Everett Gould. Grandpa Stanley died when my Dad was 18 and when he was dying, he called the family together and told them that Dad had the most level sense and so was to head the family. Well, it seems that Everett Gould was a bully and he beat his kids and his wife, Aunt Sadie. So, the Head of the family gathered four or five of his brothers and went to Everett Gould and told him that if he ever beat any of his children or his wife, they would beat him up. It was at the time of the big rush into Oklahoma. So, he took his family and his wife and fled to Oklahoma. No one knew for years that was where they were. Well Sadie and Everett are long ago dead and Mrs. Davis was one of their grandchildren and she wants to know all about the family. I have tried to help her with and she seems to be very nice but the Stanley Family did have a longing to visit other Stanleys but Mrs. Davis knew a lot about our Grandmother Stanley whose maiden name was Johnston. And I have a lot about the family history and she wants every word. She would like to come visit but I cannot have her as a guest for they are more Johnston (Grandmas maiden name.)

This has been a little look into the family past.

Being into a person's 90s is no joke but I will try to keep laughing

With Love from GG"

Lynnette may be housebound but there's a ton of activity whirling around her it seems. This is par for Lynnette. She's never bored nor boring as her world is SEEN.

The 18th of October:

"To my dearest ones Rose and Lyn:

This is the story of how I was given my name Lynnette.

Once upon a time, in 1874 to be exact, The United States decided to help any soldier that served in the Civil War who had served on the Union side Land in either Kansas, Nebraska or Oklahoma. So too was in 1874 Jehu Stanley came from Indiana with his family; Johnny who was his son by his first wife (She died during the War) And then he married Mary Jane. They had four children Rudolph, David, Norah, Sadie. They all arrived early in the month of April and lived in a dugout that Jehu had built or I should say dug out of a hillside. And on the 27th of April Mary Jane gave birth to a son, Arthur Jehu. I must here complement the lady for this was her fifth and she was to give birth to twelve more children. Jehu had promised Mary Jane that he would build her a home and though he had to travel to Lawrence Kansas for the lumber by the summer Arthur was six they were able to move into their home. Now the Stanleys were an educated family. In Indiana Jehu's Uncle had helped to build a University which today is still active. So, he talked to his neighbors and together they build a schoolhouse where all eight years were taught. The same neighbors, knowing that they did not have enough of any one church to build one for each, they all went to Topsy school and held services until they were able to build for each religious group.

And then, again at Topsy they gathered all the books they could and had a Literary Society. And one of the members of the Society was Arthur Jehu Stanley who was a teacher at Topsy. And who were members? Laura and Carolyn Elizabeth Anderson. They were my Aunt Laura, she was as redheaded as you, Rose, and my Mother called Bessie altho she was named Carolyn

Elizabeth. Then came spring, and books about love and then xxxly Arthur and Bessie were reading, I think it was Walter Scott's Idols of the King. And in this book is the love story of Gareth, one of King Arthur's knights who loved a Lady Lynnette. And during the time Arthur and Bessie were reading it they decided that their first daughter Lynnette would be the perfect name. Well, it did not work out just that way for they had a son who of course should be name Arthur. First child was a boy and of course named for his Father Arthur Jehu. And next born were twins, a boy and a girl. The boy was named for his Mother's brother Warren and Rudolph for his Father's oldest brother. Then along came me and I was at long last named Lynnette after Lord Gareth's Lady love and Eleanor for my Grandma Stanley's Mother (I forgot to write that the twin girl was name Juanita Ramona, there was a book about Ramona) and they decided that Lynnette would not go very well with Warren.

And after Lynnette came there was a wait of five years and Elizabeth Jeannette was born. She was a lovely little girl, curly auburn hair and big blue eyes, but when she went to high school she became Jean. And next there was after three years Rose Anderson Stanley was born. Beautiful red hair and big brown eyes. In her teens she was called Kansas City's Clara Bow after a famous movie star.

I did not write that the boy twin died when he was about six months old.

And this is how the name Lynnette came into our family. Two young people riding behind a horse in a buggy after a meeting of the Literary Society home very slowly and all filled with the story of Chivalry in days of yore and he proposed and she said yes.

Of the family: Arthur Jehu the First and Bessie are gone, death has come to Warren, Juanita has joined him, Jean and her husband, and their daughter Stanley husband too. Roses husband Gene, and Lynnette's Les are gone too. Arthur and his wife Ruth are still living. They have four daughters. Carolyn has been a widow for several years, the youngest of their children's husband was killed in an automobile accident just las week. My husband Les McBratney died in 1957.

And with this sketch of families and Love I am still your Lynnette the First."

"...Lynnette the First." In Game of Thrones lingo that would be: Lynnette, First of Her Name! Her Leo fire may be banked but it is far from going out. To know the origins, the story is empowering those that follow.

In November she writes:

"Dear Lyn and Jay:

So glad to hear from you and to know that you liked the story of our name. Sean's wife wrote me a lovely letter and enclosed snapshots of the two Great, great grandchildren and also a picture of all four of them. Such a beautiful family. And Lynnette-Marie who is adorable, especially the dimples. I show the pictures to everyone who comes to see me. Now this makes me GGG doesn't it?

I think it was about noon when you were born for I was there, not in the delivery room but outside biting my nails. And then I went home and called Jim and it was morning out there in California.

I hope that Cathy and Tim get their overseas commitment for it can be a good experience. I hope that Jay's Mother continues to respond to the treatment. If she is like most of the elderly persons, I know she will like the attention she must be receiving. There are fewer and fewer people in their 90's as I am living now. I am lucky to be able to get around with more than a cane. I seldom leave the house. I went to see my brother a couple of weeks ago. To get either to their back or front doors. They have so many steps from the public sidewalk to their doors. He is now 95 and confined to a walker. His wife has some spinal ailment and has to use a walker also. Carolyn their daughter does not live with them but cares for them. She said she was thinking of installing traffic lights because they keep bumping into each other. She is wonderful. She finds time to come see me as often as she can. Susan Art and Ruths youngest daughter who lives in South Carolina lost her husband two weeks ago in a traffic accident. She has decided to stay in South Carolina. They have one son who is in the military.

And now for my bad news. My son Tom's wife Mary Catherine died two years ago and since her death Tom has lived alone in their home. They had three children, Thomas Carey (names after himself and your Grandfather's best friend. He is your age and when you were little if we bought something for either of you each got the same unless the fact that one was a girl, one a boy. They there is Debra who is the something or other (I can't think what the title is) at a Museum and Art then there is Kevin. My son Tom was very active in tow things. He was retired. He was 67 years old. One of his interests was guns. The other was the St Andrews Society which was an organization of people of Scottish descent. He was a drummer in their Bagpipe and Drum Corps. Our family, the McBratney were descended from the Gailbrath family. When Mary was buried one bagpiper was at the grave and played.... I can't think just the title of the song but it was beautiful. (I forget so many things now that I am so old)

Now Kevin the youngest son had a home of his though he has never married, Tom Carey also had his own home and three children now all adults. So, my Tom preferred to live alone. Kevin went to see him at least every third or fourth day. And a week ago Tuesday he went and though he had a key, his Dad had shot the bolts on the door. It is a very old house built I the later 1800's by Mary's Grandfather and Kevin could not get in so he called the police and they broke in and found him dead. At first, they thought he had been murdered for there have been several such things in KC. He had been four days and the autopsy showed that he was a diabetic and heart troubles and a heart attack killed him. No one knew of his health problems. His bodies condition was so bad that he had to be cremated. They had a ceremony for the family only at the cemetery with the bagpipe playing the same music that he had for Mary and then there was a program at the mortuary. Debra was at a meeting in Wisconsin but came as soon as they could reach her. Jack came from San Jose. Bunnie did not come with him for she is having some trouble that made her unable to come.

I realize that my time here on earth will not be much longer but I am hoping that when I go all of my loved ones may have solved their disagreements and all the problems are forgiven. I love you and yours very much—you are my first-born Grandchild-Grandmother"

The last paragraph is giving me pause, and so is the opening to both my husband and myself. After having corresponded with her for over three decades, I can see the seeds being laid.

Chapter 13
1997, Part One

Nothing is received in the month of December, yet another reason, a different reason that I am given pause. She is again addressing her correspondence to both of us. Apparently, I had written in December and she is mentioning that she is behind in her correspondence.

The firing of the doctor is mentioned. She will mention later, that one of the reasons for the firing has to do with the doctor speaking directly to Leslie and not to her. Leslie is a retired nurse. It would appear that there are potential mental problems going on here as well.

Postmarked 28 Jan 97:

"Tuesday

Dear Lyn and Jay: I am so glad that Jay's Mother has entered a Senior Citizen Home. I had worked, as a volunteer and found that many people are happy there after they have been there for a while.

We are in the midst of winter with yesterday lots of snow about 14" on our street. We have had to be shoveled out four times lately. Today we have sunshine and the yard is as smooth as cake frosting.

I must use the pen because I was under the weather a few days and left my typewriter uncovered by the window and I guess the best description is that the ribbon cooked and will not print. As the weather is so bad I haven't been able to take it for repair.

I had a lovely letter from your Sean's wife with pictures of the children. The baby I call Dimples to myself. Both are lovely.

I went to another Dr Friday. I had fired the one I have had for three or four years. He was supposed to be so great. Well, he would not answer any of my questions concerning the treatments he was giving me so I just fired him. But now I have a very good Doctor who listened and finally I am feeling better and not like a walking drugstore.

I have a huge stack of letters to answer as well as Christmas cards. As I am now 92 years old and somewhat frail, I am trying to get my belonging s sorted out—just who gets what when I am no longer here. My brother and his wife are doing the same. He is 95 and both are now having to use walkers. They had an elevator put in so they can go upstairs. She is 3months older than I. Carolyn lives a few blocks from where they do and takes care of them a lot. Her son, daughter in law and grandson live in Denver, her daughter and granddaughter live in Sacramento. Susan the youngest of Art & Ruth's four daughter's husband was killed in an accident where a car hit him near their home in North Carolina.

You know that my son Tom had died. His wife Mary Kay had been gone a couple of years and he still lived alone in their home. His son Kevin kept tabs on him and one-day Tom was not at home and his care was not their either so he thought his Dad had gone on a trip as he often did. A few days later he went past but could not get in although the car was there, so he called the police and they broke down the door and found Tom. He had been dead a few days. He had a heart attack. None of us knew he had heart trouble. He had to be cremated and is buried beside his wife.

Jack and his son Sean I guess are both in the flood area of California. I have not heard from either for two weeks and I watch the weather reports. They are terrible everywhere.

I probably wrote you that about a year ago Debbie's husband died. She was here just after Xmas. She is still in charge of a museum & art gallery and on a state committee.

I miss seeing you two for I do care an awful lot as I always have. From what I have guessed you have been angry with me. I have loved you from the time of your birth and for all times what I wrote to you was not a scolding only my unhappiness that you should have troubles and <u>my</u> hatred of those who hurt you. I have all of your life, Lyn, tried to do things for you to make your life better. But I suppose this letter will just make you angrier of me. So be it for all I have tried to do is make life better for you.

Who knows this may be the last I will write to you. I am not sure. <u>But</u> I really have nothing to live for and only pray that I will not be here very much longer.

With Love to Jay and Yourself

Grandmother"

Well, it would seem that I am now back to keeping copies of my side of the correspondence:

"February 2, 1997

Dear Grandmother,

I am not angry with you. I do want to see you. However, it is difficult for me to do. I am going to break my own rule at this point, and attempt to discuss this even though I fear it may lead to some kind of rift with you and I again. It is not an easy topic for anyone concerned.

For years I felt Leslie to be a victim too. For years I felt that she could do no more than she had done. In the meantime, I am studying…. I study psychology, religion, metaphysics, sociology, anthropology…. I keep searching for answers to questions—questions I haven't even formulated consciously yet. All this time I am in pain, mental pain. Pain, I don't understand. At this time, I think it is related to all the ups and downs in my life. I struggle on. I keep learning. All the time my emotions are interfering with my ability to learn, my ability to grow—I am in a constant battle mode within myself. To some degree this is still going on, but it is subsiding—I can see that it might stop someday—I am working on it.

Often, I have felt like a gigantic black hole that will never be filled. What Sam did to a child was to rob her of her belief in herself. Even when I accomplish, part of me says it is a chance happening, a fluke. He left me with an immense distrust of my own voice. He would say love and then strike me, etc. Had I been older, with my personality in full development, I don't believe he would have had a chance in hell of touching me in any way. But my personality was in its formation stages. I was still learning right and wrong, reality and make-believe, etc.

But prior to Sam.... Do you not remember Leslie <u>stating that she stopped hitting me</u> when we were in West Virginia because I was in a corner of a room and she was about to strike me when I looked up at her? How old was I then? The people who abuse children, often find other abusers. Before Sam, there was Leslie. After Sam, there was Leslie; only I did not consciously realize it. With Leslie, I am totally ignored/neglected until she needs something. Usually, it was to have me reassure her that she was a good mother/person and for me to wait on her hand and foot.

Leslie often has stated that I attempt to control her life. It is a ridiculous statement. Ridiculous, until you realize that the truth, she is stating is that she desires to run my life. She wants to control me and I will have none of it. The last great example of this was when she came up to Omaha last. For two days I bombarded her (I have never ever been so nasty with anyone else in my entire life as I was with her for those 2 days), and she primarily just sat there. I guess she thought that all she had to do was listen and that I would simply run out of steam. She wasn't taking me seriously. She wasn't listening to what I was saying because each time she got a word in edge wise it was always something about how her life had been so messed up, how she was not to *blame—which translates into <u>I cannot be held responsible for anything in my own life, I am so powerless, everyone else has always controlled me, it's Lynnette's fault, it's Sam's fault, it's Lyn's fault and the list goes on and on.</u> And yet, she comes to my door uninvited, knowing I am extremely angry and why I am angry, knowing it will be extremely difficult to turn away someone at my door (although, I've gotten over that 'problem' thanks to her discourtesy). She does not want to be a parent for me, she does not want to be my friend, she does not want to be my peer. She wants to own me. She wants me to see the world only through her belief system—I must remember the past as she remembers it; I must believe as she believes or else I must belong to some strange, mysterious cult…. She has never once said she was sorry. Heaven forbids she could possibly ever be held responsible for anything that's gone wrong in her life. And you'd best remember it's <u>HER LIFE, THE REST OF US ARE EXTRANEIOUS CHARACTERS, STAGE HANDS IF YOU WILL</u>. Just writing this has caused my emotional system to go into orbit!!!*

If I physically come to see you, even if Leslie is not there…. Every morning, I have to look into a mirror and see her in my own face. I have no mother; I have no father. I do have the Universe, you, Jay, the kids…. There is no remedy here. The only choice/option I have is to admit to myself that there is no remedy. Leslie will only work over me, under me, or around me—she will not work with me to get this thing resolved. She has on several occasions informed me that I am too intelligent for her to argue with. After all these years this is probably the only true statement I remember being uttered from her lips.

Perhaps if I had healed myself faster (and I still consider this process to be an ongoing one); perhaps if I had learned faster; perhaps, perhaps, perhaps…. I can't 'fix' this, Grandmother. The fixing requires two sets of hands. Even with all my 'intelligence' I still only have one set. Perhaps someday she'll come to understand that it isn't intelligence that's required, but honesty. Regardless, I am at a dead-end. I can do no more, unless I desire to be used.

Let me think a bit more on coming down to see you. Perhaps some arrangement can be made to see you in a setting other that where you live. I do not feel comfortable with asking Leslie to leave her own home. I do not consider that to be courteous no matter how much I dislike her at the moment.

Please know that I love you."

Postmarked 10 Feb 97, just eight days after I composed and posted my last letter.

"Friday

My dearly beloved First Grandchild: I have oh so carefully reread your letter and realized how little I understood some things. You were born while you Mother was living with us. As she had called us and now, I realize we were used as a refuse. Not only that time three other times. For she knew your Grandfather and I would not have been so easy to use. I am now living with her and understand many things I did not realize. She is my child, my firstborn my baby who now I realize how often she has used not only me but my love, my husband. I miss him terribly even now. He would not have stood for the things that have been going on.

Please destroy this as soon as you read it. I have learned that she really does not care much for me but is using me. But I know what has formed her character. She inherited it....no one matters but what she wants and she is a niece of a duplicate, her Aunt Irene. They only consider themselves.

The letter I wrote you that made you so mad at me YOU misunderstood...in no way did I blame you for the ugly things that happened to you. What I was trying to say was that if I had known while you were in Germany if I had known I could have stopped it because the whatever he is called was in charge of the whatever Americans armed forces was a friend of my brother. They had worked together some time before, as Arthur mentioned when he had asked me about where Leslie and her family were in Germany. And I would have had

Arthur make contact with him and it would have cooked mister child abuser. You did not understand. And Never have I been angry at you. Never I repeat.

I shall continue to live with her until either she or me will be dead. I expect it will be me for I am now 92 ½ years old… have had three heart attacks… fired my heart specialist because he would not answer questions, I hah but talked to Leslie because she was a nurse and would understand. Am now going to another Doctor who listens to what I have to say. Bye the Doctor I fired got into serious trouble and fled before long after I fired him. Not because of me for I made no charges against him but others did.

About seeing each other. Perhaps I can come to see you and Jay. There is no bus out of Leavenworth unless they have started at least a bus stop but I could leave from Rose's. When it is a little better weather wise.

News about the family.

Arthur and his wife, who is the same age as I are having both to walk with WALKERS. They have a woman who lives nearby who is coming every day to care for the house and their meals. They have one of those elevators that consist of a strong rail up or down and a seat attached that folds flat against the wall when not in use. Carolyn lives near them and does a lot for them but she often goes to Sacramento to be with her daughter and granddaughter. Her daughter is divorcing her husband because of drinking and drugs. Her son lives in Denver and she spends some time with them. Their little boy was born with something wrong and they have just the past two-month to operate. He is three. Susan, Art and Ruth's youngest daughter who lives in North Carolina, her husband was killed when he was struck by a drunk driver. Connie their daughter who's wedding to with us have all either of their family now have home of their own so they are enjoying being alone she and Sherman.

Did I write you that my youngest son died. Tom. His wife Mary Catherine had died a couple years ago and he stayed in the home alone. He was retired and made a few trips and his younger son checked on him every three or four days. He thought his Dad was on another trip when he checked one day and his car was gone too. Then four days later he went there and could not get in. The car was there. So, he called the police and they broke in and found him dead. A heart attack. None of us knew he had a bad heart or diabetes. He must have come home just after Kevin was there for, he was in such a bad condition he had to be cremated. His daughter Debbie is still in Indiana, she is in charge of a museum and art gallery and on the state board of same. Carey the other son is still working for the Water and Light of KCK. A good position. His family are all grown and on their own.

Someday I will write you a letter all about the lady who has pink calling cards. She lives in Oklahoma and is a grandchild of my Dad's older sister. A lady with lots of nerve. And on this writing of your desire to know I leave you with much love and hoping for your understand GG

PS, Please send me Sean & wife's address. I seem to have lost it.

PS; I read thru this and discovered that I am not what I used to be…so please just laugh at the mess I have made and remember that I need your LOVE."

I read these letters now and I can see the obvious mental deterioration. It is painful for me to realize that I know that I did not take into account my Grandmother's reality. Not having laid eyes on her for so long, consumed with my own needs, I did not approach her inability to continue to do battle in this arena. I ignored it, plain and simple. I ignored it, and plowed right on ahead….

"February 16, 1997

Dear Grandmother,

It will not be necessary for you to hop the bus to Omaha. I will come to you. Unless I hear otherwise from you, I will be there Friday, 7 March somewhere between 10:30 a.m. and Noon. I will be leaving about 6-7 p.m. that same day. Jay will not be with me this time.

The main reason he will not be coming is because he is not certain of how he might handle an interaction with Leslie. The last time Leslie was here, he was upstairs during the two day 'ordeal' between her and I. I did not tell him to go upstairs, he felt then and feels now that it is best that the interactions occur without his presence. He sends you his love and respect.

I am not requesting that Leslie leave her own home. She does need to know however that if she wants to "start something," I am quite capable and willing to make the last gauntlet she ran with me look like a cakewalk! I am not necessarily proud of some of my commentary from the last fiasco with her, but…. Not much has changed except my opinion of her has lowered from the 'experience.' I am not fond of cowards. Whether their names be Sam, Leslie, or Jim.

There have been many areas of my life I have felt confused about. I am still learning and hopefully healing as I go. There are many things I have done that I'm not particularly proud of, but I take responsibility for my life and have low tolerance for those who do not.

I also have an excellent memory for those who over the years have repeatedly shown me that they do indeed love me. You have been a constant source of that love, Grandmother. Even when I have been deeply angered with you, I have always felt loved by you. When you say, 'I love you,' I believe your words."

The letter is postmarked 22 February 1997:

"Saturday

Lyn: I wonder if it would be best if you should come. You both feel so much hatred that I would probably die if either expressed your feeling. I am not making a choice but you make a threat in the third paragraph.

I do love you and would like to see you, to touch you, to kiss you. So, I cannot feel that it would be best for you to come.

I pray and ask Him why I am forced to make such a decision. If I were in better health, I would come but I cannot. And feeling as you do—you must not come.

Even though you seem not to believe it so—I do and always have done so. Loved you very much GG"

"You both feel so much hatred...." Nope. I love you Lynnette but I don't lay down arms when a known enemy enters the ring.

Chapter 14
1997, Part Two

I send no more letters. I am furious. It is not until April that I write. The letters are to myself because I feel that there is no longer anyone to write to.

"Sunday, April 13, 1997

Many years ago, I believed that once Leslie and Lynnette reconciled their differences, differences that Leslie kept assuring me they had, differences which obviously do exist, but exactly what they are I still don't know, other than it had something to do with not measuring up to another's standards, and that these differences had something to do with the reason why she wasn't a good Mother because after all her Mother never mothered her but then she had a wonderful childhood.... The sentence I started was to end somewhere, but this just keeps going in circles.

What I had started to express was that I believed that once the two of them came to an understanding with each other, then Leslie would feel comfortable enough to be able to finally confront and work through with me on this. Why and how I came to that conclusion presently alludes me, for I can find no logical pathway to it.

Perhaps I simply required that Lynnette know. Well, now she does and instead of my mother being somehow jarred into understanding her part in the scheme of things, I now lose my grandmother. I no longer want a relationship with either, for they have willed to continue their pattern and I want no part of it. I plan on living my life, not giving my life over to two people who know nothing of life other than one of us serves and the other is waited upon.

Had Leslie felt comfortable and safe in discussing her personal life with her mother; had Lynnette been more aware of her daughter's needs, had both women been more mature; had they not constantly been in competition with one another (this one is most certainly true as it is the one thing most heartily denied by both); perhaps I would have stood a chance.

Instead, they left me defenseless—battered, raped, and psychologically beaten down. I am quite sure that they have no idea of the battle I have had to wage for the last 30 years because of their inability to be a team. I am quite sure they haven't a clue as to what this stupidity of theirs has cost me. They remain quite ignorant. Ignorance is not the same as innocent.

What seems to have occurred is that both Leslie and Lynnette were speaking the truth about each other. If I take what Lynnette has stated about Leslie and what Leslie has stated about Lynnette...the confusion begins to make sense. Actually nonsense, bullshit and a whole slew of other descriptive.... One thing is certain, Leslie certainly was correct in repeatedly telling me that I did not want to tell Lynnette because her reaction would not be one that I would care for. Perhaps when the both of them are through pointing the finger at the other, they might get around to me. Perhaps they already have.

They haven't the courage to face each other alone. They proved that to me over and over again through the years. Always talking behind each other's back to me. Leslie's doing this, Lynnette is doing that. No, I am quite sure I am about the only thing they agree on these days—Lyn is off the deep end, that's for sure.

Still, even as I materialize these thoughts in writing, I am in pain. Pain, I have no real comprehension of. I hurt and it is related to these two. Why, I don't know. There is no admiration of them left. No fond memories. Only the pain.

The other day a woman had two front teeth knocked out by her significant other on our front door step. We have since found out that it has happened before. She has had offers of help. She has had the police involved. She keeps going back to the situation. She keeps getting hit. The two children she has, who are not even old enough for kindergarten, witness. One is a boy. One is a girl. She's the constancy in their world.

The little boy is learning that it is okay to strike if you are angry and the little girl is learning that she'd best not rock the boat with any male. There is no solution because nothing is faced. No courage to produce the necessary change.

I guess I'd best work on finding mine. None of this waste makes sense to me. I do know that I have had enough of it.

Addendum 4/18/97 a letter has arrived….

"Wednesday

Dear Lyn: I know that you are angry and upset by my last letter in which I wrote you telling you that I thought it best for you not to come the 9th. But you by saying that, in meaning it seemed to me, that you were coming all armed to quarrel. For what you wrote seemed to me not because you cared for me but because you felt that your fight with Leslie had not been completed and you were all loaded for the next battle. I am not taking sides and in fact I am somewhat upset about the whole thing.

I will be 93 my next birthday. I am old and while I am up and about it is mostly my will power that keeps me so. I do not want any sympathy; all that I hoped was to be loved by my family. Coming from a family where we all cared for each other, I married into a family where quarreling was daily and hatred also. Finally, I went to my Mother who as a brilliant, loving person and she said to me that no matter what was said or done to remember the truth was within myself and I could keep all the troubles, but to be forgiving and not allow hatred and troubles grow within me…. any way I took her advice and before long I was friends with them and in complete control of myself. I loved my husband very much as he did me, I tried when he was no longer with me, to help all of my children and the grandchildren. Do you think that caring for my grandchildren, as I did all of them when crisis occurred was what I wanted to do?

If you can face the fact that I love all of my children and miss Tom who died a few months ago, and that each and every one of my grandchildren are beloved by me...that is the truth. You of all should know that for you were my first grandchild.

You may have thrown this away and you may feel that it is none of my business. I am not trying to bring you and Leslie together again. That is up to you two. I am gradually going blind. This is not a sympathy notation, just a fact. I want nothing from you or your Mother. I feel very sorry for Jay for you cuddle with your anger and facts. You are perhaps cheating yourself as well him. Wake up and become the lovely person you should be.

I really do love you, just look over the past and review a few things.... I am NOT trying to tell you what to do but tell you that I LOVE you no matter what and will for the rest of my life... but you, your enemies or friends having nothing to do with that fact and that I am asking absolutely nothing from you.

With LOVE GG"

The following was written, but <u>never sent</u>, a few days later:

"Saturday, April 19, 1997

About four years ago a friend of mine said to me something I thought was rather strange at the time. She said, 'I feel sorry for them. They will never know you.' What I felt was strange was the use of the plural. 'They' and 'Them.' I have always known that this might not end up as I had hoped. This point has been a long time in coming, but it is finally here.

I was very much taken by surprise when I received your letter letting me know I should not come to see you. But the surprise was not what one might expect it to be. I was surprised because my emotional reaction was one of relief. I was relieved that I wasn't coming. I did not want to see Leslie. I did not want to see you.

I have accumulated quite a pile of correspondence and notes from the last three years—for the last 25 actually. It makes fascinating reading. Unlike most of my time relating to you two, these 'conversations' cannot be changed by what you think you said, or what she thinks she's said…it's all right there in writing. I have kept copies of my correspondence to both of you; this one will also be included. It's to become part of <u>my</u> family record.

7/21/94 'No matter how you decide this will be the last time I shall write…'

12/11/95 'This is the last time you will ever hear from me….'

1/22/96 'You will not be bothered by another letter.'

5/11/96 'this is the last time you will hear from me….'

If you love me, you will never communicate with me again."

That last line has a rhythm and content to it all too familiar and I am not happy about it. They say the sins of the Father are visited upon the sons. What of the sins of the Mother? Am I to be like her? Am I to be like so many who say one thing and do another? It hurts to think so and to see it in my own writing is excruciating.

Still….

"Sept 1, 1997 Dearest Lyn and Jay (that is if you want Jay to read this letter)

My time on earth may be short but I wanted you to realize one thing…. I have always loved you very much and gave you time that I could have with your Grandpa. We both gave up a lot trying to make your life a better place. I don't know where we went but we surely did while trying to make our daughter's life better. And thru that we must have ruined your life. I am now 93 years old and surely, I won't live much longer, for there is no happiness for me.

Much has happened to me.... My son's wife Mary died and with all three of his children were adults and able to care for themselves. He stayed in the home he and Mary Kay had lived in for years and the boys checked a few times a week as he was retired. Then he had another heart attack. He had never told them or me that he was not well. He died alone and it was several days before they knew he had gone.

Jack and his family are doing very well. But I think my only daughter hates me. She could not live as she does if there was not someone to help and manage things.

And you wrote me that you would not come see me unless we did things your way. Whatever that is. The baby, the girl I always adored dictated to me what I could or couldn't do. In no way would I at any time in your life tried to dictate to you. And even though I cry in bed at night and though you do not return the feeling I have always had for you....

This is the last that you will ever hear from me.

I hope that somewhere, somehow you realize that you were the dearest person in my world.

Your GRANDMOTHER"

Chapter 15
1998-99, The Last Letters

There is silence until a year later I receive this from Leslie:

"15 Sept 1998

Lynnette—

PLEASE READ THIS—information some of which you may want to know.

1996 Charles died

Aunt Mary K died

1997 Uncle Tom died

Your Grandmother is now 94 and has at times a short memory loss. She still is able to care for herself and move about except she has to use a cane when going outside the house. She often thinks of you and wonders what happened. If you can find it in your heart to contact her. You were the first and she loves you very much.

Please excuse the handwriting I have become shaky.

If you ever need me—you know where I am.

Love

Mother"

Breaking news! Your abuser died two years ago!

No Christmas cards in 1998, but about three months later I hear again from Lynnette:

"January 15, 1999

My very dear first grandchild:

I rather expect that you think that I side with Leslie as I have not written to you for a long while. That is not true. I feel that she has hurt herself with the things she says and does. I do not know what caused the quarrel between you—I do not want to know—Each of you are my very much-loved daughter and granddaughter.

I am now 94 years old and am expecting that my death with be in a year or so. I shall welcome it very much. I am a very lucky person—I can feed, bathe and dress myself. I walk with a cane so that I will not fall. I still can cook and keep house. So, I have not very much to complain about.

I would like very much to see you before I die. That is if you want to see me. I am working on my will---not that I have much to leave in world things.

Would you like to have the bed and dresser with the hand carved drawer pulls? If so, it will be yours. Debbie wants this old desk.

And there are a few other things—some are quite small—like the necklace my mother had made for me when she and Dad visited Mexico. At that time men made the necklaces from silver and his own designs—made on the sidewalks. Mother had one made for each of her daughters. Only Rose and I and Arthur's wife Ruth are still living. Juanita and Jean have both been dead for some time. Rose is confined to her home—se is connected to 60 feet of tubing that contains oxygen so that she can live. My brother Arthur and Ruth his wife are so ill that they have to have what is called 24 hours attention. My health is really remarkable.

The affairs in Washington DC are on TV. I do want to hear all of it. So, hoping you want to hear from and maybe see me that you still love me—

Grandmother

(I think I could make the trip to Omaha.)"

Once again, the invitation to see her is given. At this point I am just shaking my head at both of them.

The envelope is postdated Jan 22 99, seven days after the last was written:

"Friday

Dear Lyn,

Although you have not answered my letter to you, I am trying to get them to you. You were my first grandchild and I loved you then and so do now.

I am trying to make assignment of the few things that I have because there are only a few more years at the best for me to live. I was born August 6, 1904.

And I would like for my Grandchildren to leave the things that I have. For instance, the desk where I now write. My son Tom's daughter will be happy to get this. Tom and his wife died about a year apart 4-5 years ago. My son Jack and his wife Bunny are still alive and so are their five children—all in California. Tom & Mary Kay left three children.

My sister Rose is very ill. She has to remain in her home and has to keep her 60-foot oxygen attached to her—heart trouble.

My brother Arthur (who is 3 years older than I) and his wife Ruth are in 24-hour care—both of them—Ruth is my age which makes it very hard for her as she is helpless. Arthur retired about 3 years ago—He had been a Federal District Judge for several years.

I do love you dearly and wish you were near enough so I could see you.

With sincere Love Grandmother"

Five months later, postmarked 6-18-99:

"*Thursday*

Dear Lynnette:

It has been two years or more since I have tried to get in touch with you. I am still living with your Mother in Lansing. This will be the last time that I will be in touch with you unless you wish it.

I am now in my 90's (in age that is) but strangely I am able to take care of myself. I am the oldest person in our neighborhood and can still walk.

The reason I am writing you is that years ago when I bought the bedroom set with the carved drawer pulls—you liked it so much I think I said you could have it someday. Well someday is coming rather fast and I am now making out my will. Now I do not have or ever had much in the way of worldly things. My income will not exist after I am gone. But there are some things—like that bedroom set—that I want certain persons to have—if they want them.

Unless I make this will my daughter Leslie will take everything. I am going to a lawyer make out the legal will and will send copies (if I live long enough) to all my descendants.

You were my first grandchild. Believe it or not I have adored all of my grandchildren. I do not know of any great grandchildren.

I probably will never see any of you again. Your Uncle Tom and his wife Mary Catherine both died within a short time of each other.

Of course, you and Mac are your Mother's children. Mac is married but does not have children, but step children now adults.

Jack and his wife Bunnie have five children. The oldest girl has two daughters—they were in college this year.

Enough of our family.

But for my family—Rose (who is a widow) lives alone in the house where you all visited me several years ago. She has severe heart problems and cannot leave the house. My brother Arthur lives here in Leavenworth. He is the oldest of my family. He is now 98 years old. His wife Ruth is my age. They are both in what is called here Home Care—People come and care for them instead of their being in the Hospital. Arthur was for almost 20 years the Federal Judge for this district. My sister Juanita has been gone (dead) for several years. So Rose, Arthur and I are all left of our family. Oh—I forgot to write that my sister Jean has been dead for several years. I do not think you ever met her. She did not live in Kansas City.

This has been a book—sorry.

Leslie and I live here in Lansing which is a small town attached to Leavenworth. About three weeks ago Leslie had an accident and now we do not have a car—luckily, she was not hurt, and she says she does not want to drive anymore. I started driving when I was about 16 (boyfriend taught me) and until I came here, I had a car of my own. When I lived on the east coast and when I lived on the west coast. I did use Rose's car as long as I lived with her but I have not driven a car for years now. So, we are dependent on the taxi service or friends.

This has become a book—so this is enough.

I love you very much although it has been years since I saw you, My first grandchild.

Your loving Grandmother

Lynnette McBratney"

It's becoming more and more apparent that her mind is not what it was. She is mis-remembering people and places and time periods. Even if I chose to see her, the odds are that it would only destabilize an already, precarious home scene.

In this next letter, a letter is mentioned. It is postmarked about a month and a half from the last letter I received. I suspect that what she received was a Baby Announcement from our Daughter as another great-great-granddaughter was born the 16th of July in Germany.

Postmarked the 29th of July:

"My dear Lyn:

I was so glad to hear from you. And just who are the parents of Kira Morgen? She must be as near perfect—almost 9lbs, and 21 inches tall. She will be lovely as a child and as an adult.

Leslie and I are doing very well here in Lansing. Leslie is retired and I have been for a long time.

O my family—My brother Arthur and his wife. Who is exactly my age. And Rose the youngest of my family are all that are alive of all of us. My brother and his wife and I live near each other. Rose lives in Kansas City, Kansas—alone. We all stay in contact.

I am sorry I have not seen you more than I have. And as I cannot travel anymore, I probably will not see you again. Always remember that I sincerely do love you. As I am 95, I know I shall not be around very much longer.

There will be no inheritance for I have not been wealthy. However, at one time you said you would like the bedroom furniture—the set that has the hand carved drawer pulls. If you still would like to have it you shall. I still walk, talk, care for myself in every way, and write my own checks.

I am sending a check for Kira (What a good name, I like it.)

Does she make you a Grandmother? And make me a <u>great</u> grandmother again?

Leslie is retired now. She is active in the church. She did have a car but about 3 weeks ago she was in a wreck and the car is no more. She won't let me get *her another—so we just have to use the Taxi. (Maybe I should say <u>buy</u> a Taxi—it is so expensive) Our relatives, friends and neighbors are willing to take us anywhere we have to go.*

My best wishes to Kira and all of her family.

With Love to You

Grandmother

McBratney

Please fill in the proper name on the check to make it easier to cash or deposit it.

L."

She may have realized her error in believing that I had resumed correspondence again, or she may have thought that she had actually written to her great-granddaughter. I've never known her to refer to herself as "Grandmother McBratney." If the check was there, I would have forwarded it to our daughter. I have no notation that it was enclosed.

There will be no more letters from Leslie.

There will be no more letters from Lynnette.

The written communications are over.

There will be no more letters, phone calls, rejected gifts, cards, or unexpected visits. Leslie will die on Thanksgiving Day the year prior to 9/11. It will be the brother that I've not spoken with in over a decade who calls. He'll begin that phone call by asking me if I am sitting down.

Chapter 16

Leslie's Death

The last missive was received in July 1999. A year and a half later I will hear from my brother.

From a journal entry the day after Thanksgiving in November of 2000:

"11/24/00, Friday

Mac called yesterday. I hadn't heard his voice in over 10 years. Leslie died at 8:05 a.m. Thanksgiving Day. A neighbor called over a month ago and told me that Leslie had fallen and broken her hip. She was still in the hospital when she died. So far all I know is that she woke up, became unconscious and never regained consciousness. Uncle Jack has been called, but during the holidays I am sure it will be difficult to catch a plane from California. Mac is to call again with the information regarding the funeral.

I am in a bit of a quandary. Not certain at all what I should or should not be feeling or doing. I was to be working at the store today, helping with the inevitable after-Thanksgiving crowds. Luckily, I was able to spend the holiday with Jay and his family. It was good to be surrounded by them.

I have been going over the correspondence, which has accumulated over the last seven years. 1993 was when I threw down the gauntlet. It wasn't that any of us was debating what had happened, it was that we were all debating what exactly our parts were in relation to what had happened. Here I sit amidst the pile of venom. Accusations flying left and right. Of the three of us, I don't know who hurled the least amount of venom. I suppose Leslie, but that is only because she didn't choose to communicate much.

I have notified everyone at work that I won't be in until at least Tuesday. I think I'll call Mac. He is not home, so I left a voice mail asking him to call me. I am fairly certain that everyone is at Grandmother's probably trying to make decisions regarding the funeral and so forth. I think it is time for me to take a walk.

It's a bright, sunny, cloudless day. Really pleasant for the end of November in Nebraska. As I walked a thought occurred to me that when we are dead, if everything I have been reading is anywhere near the truth, we are supposed to be able to see all things quite clearly. I thought perhaps that this might mean that Leslie is now seeing, perceiving with this clarity now. I thought perhaps that this might mean that she would say that she is sorry now—seeing with these new soul-filled, clear eyes. If my thought is correct, I am finally free to say that I forgive. Perhaps now we can have peace. Perhaps, if I have seen things with reasonable clarity all this time.... Perhaps she now sees as well. That is a lot of 'perhaps.'

I apologize to my Mother if I did not communicate to her this need for the apology. I could stand here and swear that I did try, very, very hard to communicate this to her. My heart tells me that I did. My heart also tells me that this argument is no longer valid now. There is no one to argue with. Whether I communicated this to her or not simply cannot be proven. It cannot be proven because she is dead and cannot be asked. It cannot be proven because even if she were alive our versions of reality might yet clash again.

Choice. There is always a choice. Every second of every minute of every hour of every day of our lives, there is choice.

I, Lynnette do hereby choose to believe that the quarrel between my Mother and I is ended and that we each do wish the other well. I could be wrong, but I could be right. Let it be. I pray that The Universe finally allows me an extremely clear view of this after my physical death. Goodbye, Mother."

I go for another walk the next day and my psyche lets me know this 'closure' of mine is but wishful thinking. As I walk along the path, I have made for myself for the last 20 or so years, I am thinking about our driving down to Leavenworth that afternoon. We are to be staying with Grandmother and I will be seeing her for the first time in over seven years. But my thoughts are on the funeral as I walk this particular stretch, luckily not far from home.

I am walking along the sidewalk when out of nowhere, a dog bites me. It came from behind and bit me on the back side of my thigh. My reaction is anger. I chase the dog, growling, of all things! It runs into a yard and cowers there. I bang on the front door of the house, no one answers. Noting the address, I proceed to walk back home. There's little blood or pain but that will change. As I begin to walk back, what enters my mind is that Leslie's spirit has somehow entered or made this dog bite me. So much for the closure, I was hoping for….

Our drive is delayed as I speak with police and humane society officers. The humane officer and I jokingly refer to the dog as 'The Mugger.' I get a tetanus shot and assorted medicines from the emergency clinic. We are on the road to Leavenworth around 2 p.m. Nothing is going to keep me off the road to Lynnette."

I had enough sense about me to journal during some of this time period. Beginning with that same Saturday I am bit by the dog….

Chapter 17
The Funeral

"Saturday

We arrive about 5 p.m. Mac and Dee, his third wife, are already there. GG does not recognize me. She is very cordial, and talks of how she is to move in with her sister soon. I think she means Rose, but I will later come to understand that she is actually referring to Leslie and the assisted living facility they were scheduled to move into. She goes to bed. The rest of us stay up for a while talking. Mac does most of the talking.

Dee is quite good as Mac's side-kick. He has developed quite a family unit around him. I am glad for him and glad for Leslie too for this group/crowd of his seems to have taken to her—included her in most of their lives. I am glad she had that.

Slept on the sofa. Should have taken a blanket. I'll do that tonight. We did not get to bed until about midnight. Everything is pretty much already under control here. There's really not much for me to do but putter around in the kitchen and grab snatches of conversation with GG, who pretty much stays in her bedroom.

Not much has changed at the house except for the disarray. The most glaring examples are in the kitchen. In years gone by there is no way the dishes, would be as they are now. Grandmother's patterned set (Misaka floral, white with purple and pink iris) and Leslie's patterned set (Jägermeister hunting scenes, black and white) are all mixed in with the daily use Correllware (white with a green, small daisy border) along with a mix of take-out containers. It's quite a hodge-podge.

The refrigerator has cheese and some fresh vegetables which were past their prime. I also found the percolator on with the remains almost evaporated down to where it was starting to burn. All this tells me is that there is no way Grandmother has been capable of anything for some time---I'd guess months. Who has been minding the store?

Sunday

I spent the day cleaning and cooking. I am trying to tidy the place up for Jack, my mother's oldest and last surviving brother. He and his wife arrive on Monday night.

Monday

Mac and his wife did not stop by yesterday. I suspect they decided that Mac needed some rest. He had a cold and Saturday night when they went to leave his voice was going. Jack and Bunny are to arrive today from California. Jay and I will be going into a hotel room for tonight. Grandmother is a bit unnerved—she senses something is up in relationship to her, I think.

I was able to make the thin noodled chicken soup for her yesterday. A couple of the neighbors dropped by to express their condolences and we all popped 'My Fair Lady' into the VHS to watch. Jay's been sleeping downstairs and I'm on the sofa to make sure that GG doesn't, in her confusion, go out the front door. Off and on, mostly off, she remembers who I am. The funeral is tomorrow.

Monday, again

Mac had quite a conversation with Jay. It seems, that he is pissed off at me. He told Jay that he had wanted to talk to me about everything but Leslie told him not to because he would get mad and try to kick my ass. Many other things were said to Jay along this line. Gee, I wonder where I've seen this behavior before?

Jack and Bunny came in. Possibly one of the few positive things to happen the whole time we've been here.

Tomorrow the funeral....

Tuesday

Jay and I are up and ready about 7:30 a.m. We go to MacDonald's for breakfast and then we drop by Grandmothers. I had forgotten my Franklin Planner and my sunglasses. Go up to the door and Bunny opens it. They have no water it seems. Jay checks the place out. Jack is out trying to get the bridge of his glasses fixed and doesn't know that they are without water. There's no obvious reason for the water being off so I called the Lansing Water Co. Spoke with Sandy there. Yep, the $16.43 bill had not been paid. About 10 minutes later they've waived the disconnect fee and the water is back on. Bunny hops into the shower.

We arrive at the Morman Stake just as Jack, Bunny, and GG arrive. Leslie lays in her casket. Neither of us approaches the casket. I manage to get into the chair next to Lynnette. About 30 people come and go. Lynnette introduces Jack to one of the folks there as her husband. Jack quickly sets the record straight. The service is held at 1 p.m. An hour or so later we are at the Leavenworth National Cemetery. Mac is given her flag. Jay and I exit ASAP. We are home by 6 p.m.

Prior to the time of the funeral, Grandmother became quite upset because no one had told her of the funeral arrangements for her own daughter. I spoke with Mac about it. I was concerned. Mac's response was that she had been told (which of course she had been) and now did I see what he and Mom had to put up with all these years? I was very confused by his level of anger. I remember little other than going back to be with Grandmother at the time.

Mac had abruptly reminded me that for he and Leslie, Lynnette was a burden. See what they had to endure? See what they had been put through?

All I could think of were the possible years that had now opened up to me. She may have dementia but we still easily converse. Our connection is still present even when she does not know who I am or why I am there.

When Bunny and Jack first arrived from California, that evening Jack mentioned that he was leaning toward leaving Grandmother in Leavenworth. If he did so, would I promise to come and see her?

Absolutely!"

Chapter 18
My Mother's Daughter

Prior to the funeral, Mac called me downstairs. He had a poem I had written as a child. I recognized it but I remembered little about it—it referenced a tea cup and my mother. One of those cute things a kid will do when a grade school teacher asks that you write something for your mother or father. He gave it to me. I gave it back without comment. He then shrugged his shoulders and continued his rummaging amongst Leslie's standing armoire. The only thing I wanted from that house was my Grandmother.

The poem held no meaning for me, other than it was painful that Leslie had kept it all that time. It was really a pity that what we could have been simply wasn't. Guilt? No, my heart shook the sentiment off quickly enough. Perhaps that was Mac's intent in showing it to me. He anticipated that guilt would be my response. Nope, not these days little brother.

Shortly after the birth of my daughter in 1970, I had written another poem:

> *I'm my mother's daughter,*
> *Never was no daddy's girl.*
> *I'm my mother's daughter,*
> *She brought me to this world.*
> *I'm my mother's daughter*
> *And if you think this loving strange,*
> *Remember it was always momma's arms*

That always opened when I came.

At the time I was very emotionally tied to this writing. I'd just given birth to my daughter. I was a mother for the first time. I showed it to a very talented friend of mine and she quickly came up with a tune for it. It was rather catchy.

It was also a total lie. I believed in it at the time, but there were no open arms. "And if you think this loving strange...." When I wrote this, I was just beginning my journey out of what I would come to view as the enslaved part of my life. The gist of this writing was the rejection of Sam's dominion. I even toyed with the idea of changing my last name to "Lesliechild."

Writing that I was my mother's daughter in my early twenties, I was very, very, very far from comprehending that two decades later I'd be showing her the door and that the next time I would see her, she would be lying in a coffin.

You paint me pretty pictures,
Yet the reality remains;
The memory of the child,
Within the adult,
Knows the pain.

It's a pity that we never had the calm and honest conversations that were sought. I understood more about your life than you would allow me the opportunity to disclose. Because of these writings, I understand even more. We could have been friends, but we chose a different path. Combat, war is never won. Diplomacy was the path never taken. What was needed to be learned, likely by both of us, was never given the opportunity to be born.

No doubt every time you and Lynnette had a disagreement, she would just let you blow off your steam. She'd just stand there and wait for you to expel all the adolescent energy you had built up. Not feeling that she was taking you seriously you would end up blaming her for your errors, or blaming her for the reality of how our world works. Perhaps sometimes you were even right in that regard. Either way, you would reject the outcome of these skirmishes.

She'd offer you down to earth responses that you would perceive as punishment for confiding in her. I can get that. Often when we have something that is awry in our lives the cure is a different way for us to think, or feel, or act. I get how that can be construed as punishment, especially since often all you were really looking for was a shoulder, a confidant, someone to assure you that your teen self wasn't going crazy.

You'd still be upset. The outbursts did little to change anything. Frustrated, you'd eat too much and become depressed and consequently do nothing, which further depressed you. Eventually, you simply stopped confiding in her.

Neither you nor Lynnette should have attempted that with me. Not after Sam. Not after Gary. Not after a multitude of worldly battles you knew nothing of because, like you, I did not feel I could confide or ask advice of my mother. It's not that I am too intelligent, it's that I am battle tested.

Your relationship with Lynnette was an unacknowledged competition, as only you viewed it this way. Lynnette's relationship with her mother, Bessie, was mutually constructive. Lynnette likely anticipated that her relationship with her daughter would be also. It's truly unfortunate, for all of us, that Bessie dies just a year after I am born. We all could have benefitted from the wisdom that Grandmother spoke of.

Lynnette's relationship with her in-laws, your paternal grandmother and siblings, was not constructive. The remarks, made mostly during your spells of anger with me, spoke of how your grandparents had raised you. You would speak of how Lynnette was not a good housekeeper and that she mostly read a lot. Yet, in your letter to me about your life you state that you had been raised by a loving family?

There was never mention of how Lynnette was a Red Cross volunteer and how she was one of the Rosie the Riveters, working at the Bomber North American Plant during WWII. One of the things you bemoaned, as you left my home for the last time, was how Lynnette and I ran your life. That sounded pretty weird coming from someone so close to 70 at the time.

Lynnette's remarks state that she considered you a McBratney "through and through." She said that she was reminded, from time to time, how much you resembled her mother-in-law or one of her sisters-in-law. She told me her mother-in-law had stood over her with a knife in her hand as she seemingly lay sleeping. Not good, and certainly not a sign of stability. I'm certain that your mother's comparison did not aid your relationship.

We lose a little of ourselves when we are compared to others. When the comparison is negative, it tears us down through no fault of our own. She never mentions this to you that I am aware of, but surely you must have suspected this from time to time.

While he was still in his early teens, your father had been the male supporting the family when his father died. Your mother was seen as a villain for marrying him. They may have believed she trapped him as you were born so soon after they wed. Was it two sets of grandparents that you reference as having raised you, or just the one?

Your mother and father married six years after the ending of World War I. They eloped. Your father was not truly accepted by your maternal grandparents until shortly after you were born.

The story that Lynnette told me was that her father was quite the jokester. Arthur, Bessie, and William were just outside the delivery room. Arthur was beaming at you as he held you then he pretended to drop you. William immediately dove to catch you! According to Lynnette that was your father's passport to her parents' hearts.

You would be the only daughter in this immediate family. Following your birth Jack would be born in about three years, and then your little brother Tom a couple of years after that. Yet, you would remain the first born, the apple of your father's eye and possibly, at one time, of your mother's heart as well. There's a tale of how your father almost punched out President Truman in your defense.

There's no outside-the-family verification of this, but Lynnette told of how the three of you were at a social function. It was possibly a reunion of the old unit where William had been Truman's bugler. William and Truman are conversing when you catch Truman's eye. He points you out to William and before your father can introduce you to him, Truman comments on your ample bosom. Lynnette said that she quickly stepped in to rescue the situation so that your father would not hurt his...hand.

From your own accounts there were no beaus in high school. I get that. Most people, girls and boys, get that. As adults, most of us sigh and shake our heads a bit in response to those memories. For you it seems to have been more of a personal stigma. Your personal cross to bear. James would change that belief at least temporarily. It feels good to be loved, to be in love, to be seen as someone who is worthy of love.

It must have irritated you that brother Jack, two years your junior, would jump into the Merchant Marines at 16. Newly graduated from high school, he wasn't old enough to enlist in anything else. He'd be joining the Navy a few years before you enlisted into the Navy Nurse Corps. It could be that the Navy's Nursing program was brought to your mother's attention by your eldest brother.

It would have been good to discuss this with you. We could have discussed this. All I know of your relationship with your brothers is that Tom was your favorite. Was it you and he against Jack? Did Jack become your mother's favorite?

Lynnette and William's heads must have been spinning because you and your two younger brothers would all be married by the time I am born in 1951. I will turn out to be the first of ten grandchildren born between 1951 and 1961.

I am sorry that you and James couldn't make a go of it, just as I am sorry that Gary wasn't ready for marriage and kids. (Neither you nor I were either.) I know how tough it can be as the financial head of a family unit, but I've never had to attempt to do it and be pregnant at the same time. That had to be tough, even with your parents being so close by.

James drank and Gary was a thief, both left the military earlier than they probably should have. There was nothing either of us could do about their activities. Both were never satisfied with what they had. For both of them the grass was always greener anywhere else than where they were. We bore the brunt of the fallout from their missteps. It is really hard to deal with another's missteps, especially when we've been making plenty of our own. That would bring us to Charles.

What the hell possessed you to marry him? I truly get that Lynnette can be difficult. But Sam? I know and I can only imagine what it must have been like in the mid 1950's. I certainly know what it was like in the early 80's. A divorcee with two kids is not what most males are looking for, and both of our first marriages left us financially in peril. Living on the precipice is never a great place to start while trying to raise two very young kids.

It's likely your parents had more to do with your first divorce than either you or Lynnette ever let on. Your father's death, both your brothers are married and everyone's left the nest but you. Additionally, Lynnette is trying to figure out what her first move as a widow is to be. I don't know what the answer could have been, but I do know that it should not have been him. Never him.

You could have made it on your own, and I truly get how scary attempting to do that can be! You eventually did make it on your own, but then somehow you and Lynnette decided to take up housekeeping together? That's never been a good mix for either of you.

My reasoning for getting back with Gary was that the original family unit would get back together. At least, that's what I told myself at the time. Looking back, I really question the reasons behind my getting back with him. I think it is very, very possible that it had more to do with being an adult on my own for the first time in my life. Was it the same for you? Was this your fear as well?

Oprah has said that: "Forgiveness is giving up the hope that the past could have been any different.*"[35] I truly do not know if I am ever going to forgive you for your betrayals. I know I will never forget.

As I attempt to understand your mess, as I attempt to clean up my own mess, I am reminded that our messes have affected the generations that have been born after our births. Who knows, but I believe that we would agree that it is our hope that they do better than we.

---

[35] Bruce D. Perry, M.D., Ph.D. and Oprah Winfrey, What Happened to You? Conversations on Trauma, Resilience, and Healing (New York: Flatiron Books, 2021) p. 289.

Chapter 19
The Final Trip To Kansas

"Jesus, I trust in you." The sign is planted in a farmer's field, and when we return, we'll see a similar message displayed for travelers headed north. I get very tired looking at signs. Billboards saturate the world. They are so full of the MUST, SHOULD, SHALT (the shouted must?), we truly need be concerned with the opportunities presented by the word "COULD." Could is where hope begins.

We have traveled this well-worn road many times since the death of my mother. She had been in the hospital recuperating from a broken hip, no doubt the fall was attributed to the Parkinsons diagnosis. Thanksgiving she woke up and never woke up again. After her funeral, my husband and I began visiting Lynnette on a monthly basis.

One Saturday out of four, we'd go up and back. The visits consume most of a day, but there's never been a question between us as to why we go. We don't know it yet, but Grandmother will die a few days after this visit. She is the destination. After her death, all meaningful connection to this path shall pass away as well.

A few weeks before Grandmother passed away, the nursing home had attempted to contact my Uncle in California. He became Grandmother's power of attorney when my Mother had been hospitalized that last time. Mother and grandmother had lived together for about 25 years. Mother had fallen, and it was during her stay in the hospital that the powers of attorneys had been drawn up. Jack for Grandmother and Mac for Leslie.

In the event the next fall Leslie took was fatal, her last living sibling would be able to quickly step into the role of caregiver to their mother. It was a wise action to take, as Grandmother had been mentally and physically going downhill. When my mother passed away, everything was already in place.

Jack flew in for his sister's funeral and before he returned to California, Grandmother was in an assisted living facility. Already 96 years of age, the trip from the Midwest to the Pacific coast was not realistic. However, she needed a bit more supervision than the living center was set up for. She began wandering on her own.

On one occasion, Grandmother was going to visit her younger sister in Kansas City. Rose had passed away the week before. Having smoked since early adulthood, she had been attached to an oxygen tank for some time.

Rose was a very spirited woman, and Grandmother had been able to see her briefly a few months earlier at the funeral of their eldest brother who had passed away about a month short of his 100th birthday. Stanley_bio.pdf (squarespace.com) They had not seen each other in some time. It was good to see them together, even under such circumstances.

Rose and Lynnette had been close. They had lived together for a time after Grandmother had retired from Lockheed. Rose had retired some years before. My flamboyant aunt, always the height of fashion, had been a buyer for an upper end retail chain. They were close in temperaments as well, which is probably one of the reasons Grandmother ended up living with Leslie.

Grandmother was really looking forward to the luncheon they had planned. The luncheon, she told us, that they had planned just the day before. She was transferred to a nursing home less than a year later.

It was Aunt Bunny, Jack's wife, who let us know that Grandmother was gone.

Ashes to ashes, dust to dust;
At least it means that we don't rust.
Be there a heaven,
Be there a hell—
Let's hope there's more than
The gods seem willing to tell.

I doubt that this would be perceived to be appropriate. Although, I suspect strongly that Grandmother would approve. (Privately, of course.)

She once told me, in one of those "private" conversations, that she wasn't all that certain whether God was male or female or something altogether else. She also told me that she didn't belong to any particular religion because to do so would be something akin to playing favorites among her children.

Lynnette gave birth three times. It would be just prior to their individual marriages that the two boys would become Catholic and, I think it was Episcopalian. After her second and last divorce, my mother would turn to the Mormon Church. I know she was Baptist at one point, and I believe Methodist prior to that. I'm a bit unsure, as we (i.e. my mother, my brother and I) never seemed to go to church when the husband-fathers were around.

Grandmother and I would communicate religiously throughout my life, but seldom would we converse on the subject of religion. I have always felt my time with her to be very special. Even when, before she died, her mind was not as it once was—even then, I found her endlessly fascinating.

During the five years that would follow, I learned a great deal about her that had remained unrevealed to me. After all those years of primarily written conversation, being able to see her during this stage of her life, allowed me an opportunity to be privy to much of what really was going on in that internal universe of hers.

Who would have ever guessed that she dreamed of being a star of the stage! Yet there she was, all dolled up waiting for her limousine to pick her up for that evening's performance. Luckily the attendants were on their toes. (It is a little difficult not to notice a woman wanting to go out into the heat of a midwestern summer in a full length, woolen, winter coat.)

Then, there was the time she told us that she had just returned from South America. Her company had sent her to go over the accounts. She was just glad that she had gotten back from her trip in time to catch our visit.

I miss her. I have a sense that I will never miss her, as I miss her so much.

Bunny had called to let us know that the nursing home had notified them that Lynnette had pneumonia. We were to find out later that she was hospitalized the next day. We had made plans to go see her but had already decided against it as I still had the remnants of a flu bug and had not wanted to contaminate anyone. These delays are how we came to be on the road to Leavenworth to see her just a few days before she would die.

When we arrived, she was just finishing her lunch. She had not eaten much and you could tell the staff was concerned. She had been released from the hospital 48 hours earlier and was not doing well. I could barely understand her when she told me she needed to lie down. She told us she was nauseated and tired.

We got her to her bed and she began dreaming. I held her hand, tears streaming down my face. I knew. We both knew. I had been given the opportunity to say goodbye. I got the chance to say I love you and to thank her for all she's done for me. All she continues to do. The pain is still present. She had passed a hundred years of living. She had always been in my world. The funeral, we are not attending. I want this behind us, over with, completed and filed. I want simply to move on.

The light of my life was my maternal grandmother. No matter where in the world I was, it was Lynnette who would remember my birthday. It was she who wrote and to whom I would write. She had taught me to read and to form my letters. From her I learned a respect for books and a love of reading. She was my first friend and my most constant companion. She was also a companion that I seldom had the opportunity to be physically around.

At one time, she had read a series of historical novels that mentioned a Native American tradition of naming a person to fit their actions in life. I remember her referring to me as "Little Mother of the World." My heart has always responded to her as "My Lioness."

Some time ago, she had written to me the tale of how our name came to be in the late 1800's: "And this is how the name Lynnette came into our family. Two young people riding behind a horse in a buggy after a meeting of the Literary Society home very slowly and all filled with the story of Chivalry in days of yore and he proposed and she said yes." What my great-grandparents were reading was Lord Tennyson's, <u>Idylls of the King</u>. The Lady Lynette was the love interest of the King Arthur's Knight, Gareth.

I attempted to find out how our name came to be written with two, instead of one "n", but her mind was too far-gone at age 99 to reply. On the day I asked, I believe she was at about 16 years of age. Instead of answering my query, she had replied with a question of her own: "Do you think I will ever have a beau?" She emitted a huge sigh, as her eyes shyly would not meet my own. I never ever remember my grandmother as being particularly demure, but here she was in all her teenage glory!

"Yes!", I had reliably replied to her curiously dreamy, adolescent concern. My heart wanted to say to her that she would have such a beau that all others would pale in comparison. Such was the fabled love of my grandparents.

For almost half a century she would be a widow. She never remarried. She had some respectful offers, but they were not he. I wish that I had thought to ask her earlier. It would have been a marvelous story. I never outgrew my love of her voice, nor the tales she would weave of everyday events. The world was somehow always exciting and very much worth living around her.

Lynnette always fared wonderfully with children. When those children became adults, well there was another side of her that many had difficulty with. I, too, brushed with the dark side a few times. She cared. You always knew she cared, and in that caring, sometimes she cared too much. Whatever you came to her with, she always gave you the most she had to give. Sometimes what she had to say, you simply were not ready to hear.

It was best to remember she was Leo. Never, ever forget to honor that. The Lioness had a core that demanded the royal recognition of her reign. She was not going to abdicate that throne. Even into dementia that throne was hers.

She told me that she stopped crying when grandfather was dying. He told her not to cry. Our psyches are so fragile—I am certain he did not mean for her to literally not cry anymore, only to move on with her life and to be ever so grateful for what they had meant for one another.

Until recently, I have been living a life too busy trying to stay afloat. Ironically, my grandmother tells a similar tale. A tale of obligation, of family needs, and of personal issues put to the wayside as you try to strengthen strained areas of the family. Perhaps, there is something that needs saying. Lynnette, I think, would agree.

As for Leslie…. I'm still working on it, Mother.

Chapter 20
Our Final Meeting

As Leslie left my doorway, she left a sound trail of verbal breadcrumbs. Actually, they were uttered more like closing curses, as she exited the way she had entered—without notice, finally noticing she was not welcome. After stating that she would not force herself on me, she had driven four hours to arrive on my doorstep, to force herself on me.

"I had to wait until I was 69 to find out I was a bad mother?" It was rather like the time she told me that she always feared that I would no longer trust her. She did not seem to notice that I made no reply.

Trust is not something you feel when it takes your mother six years to divorce after she is told her husband has been raping you for over a decade. No one gets points for not having sex with the enemy even as you remain in their bed. This was not information I welcomed in the first place. This was information that for some reason she felt was important for me to know? I'm still not certain why this came out of her psyche. It's not pretty, whatever it is.

The two lists that Lynnette wanted of me, had already, long ago been considered. The lists were inconclusive at best, and as I mentioned in my response, even if they had been more on the positive side, they still did not justify the abuse, the betrayals. I had determined that I had nothing left to lose as well.

After I responded by suggesting that they make the same lists of each other, their reactions were swift and outraged. How dare I! Leslie and Lynnette seldom agreed on anything but they vehemently agreed on this. Taking the knives they had been inserting for decades into each other's back they proceeded to synchronize their attack on me. At least this was a frontal attack. "Et tu, brute?"

"While trauma keeps us dumbfounded, the path out of it is paved with words, carefully assembled, piece by piece until the whole story can be revealed.*"[36] I had not thrown my gauntlet down lightly, with little thought. A great deal of agonizing went into the initial note I sent Leslie. Consider the missive to be at least a decade in the making. At least a decade in the making, before I determined I could go no further without this last-ditch effort on my part.

I had reached a tipping point. I wasn't gaining anything for the length of time, the length of care, I took. The walk of the eggshells seemed to only illicit further abuse. I was not taken seriously. I was being dismissed. I was being disrespected. I was being told to forget this betrayal, make nice only. That was never ever going to be the reality.

I knew the truth. They knew the truth. The result was going to be that every chance going forward I was going to get sniped at. Rather than direct confrontation, I'd be placed in the position of taking "indirect" hits the rest of my life. Well, at least, for the rest of my life around either of them. Ain't happening. It would have been one thing if they had never darkened my doorway again, but they just kept showing up expecting their undue due.

---

[36] Bessel Van Der Kolk, M.D., "The Body Keeps the Score—Brain, Mind, and Body in the Healing of Trauma." (New York: Penguin Books, 2014) p.234.

Let's be clear. Action speaks louder than words but, no action elicits complicit. No action breeds contempt. When the silencers have determined to burden themselves with unacknowledged guilt, they too easily begin to resent the victim.

If you chose not to silence yourself, you become the reminder of what they don't want to be reminded of. Since they seemed determined to keep darkening my doorstep, the result is passive aggression. Apparently, both my mother and my brother wanted to "kick my ass." Not particularly passive aggressive, but if it is not threatened anywhere near your ears, it is merely smoke calling itself fire.

Lynnette wanted peace at my expense. She could have donned the robes then of peacemaker. The Lioness Halo in place, she could have then become as unaware of the barbs thrown at me as she had been allowed to be made unaware of the original sins cast upon me. Passive aggressors seldom act out their venom in the presence of The Queen of Hearts. Unresolved issues find a victim and that victim was going to be me—the designated family sin-eater. When the family sins are acknowledged by only one of its members guess who gets to eat what they have sown?

No personal, human, one to one discussion. No mother-daughter conversation. No heart to heart of the pain that is felt in having our sibling relationship torn to shreds by the same villain. It's way too easy to say "I love you." If your mother says it, everyone just nods the societal prescribed *of course she does* built-in response after all, she's your mother.

Being the child of someone who has allowed their subjugation by another, means that you too have been subjugated. There can be no other reality while you are a child. My brother kept on about how we were taught to survive when what we were surviving was the situation, she not only put us in, but kept us in.

Another utterance in that doorway she would never return to was: "Have you thought about the example you are setting for your daughter?" The word "children" was not used. Only the female? Interesting but not surprising. Where there is racism, you can count sexism raising its warped head. It's all about the hierarchy—if you can't maintain your position by deed, you can shout out what you "deserve" but have not "earned."

She was throwing the last salvoes she felt she had. In her mind she equated my "disrespecting" of her with how I too would be disrespected because I was showing my daughter she could behave in this manner. You're damn right, I was!

The Thou SHALT of the Ten Commandments regarding the honoring of your mother and your father cannot be a binding contract, at least not initially. It cannot be a binding contract because a minor is not legally allowed to enter a binding contract. There are obvious reasons for this. If this contract is to come into existence at all, it is first the parent who must abide by it.

Where does she abide by it? Show me where my "fathers" abide by it? Furthermore, show me where she is honoring her contract with her own living parent? Who is setting the example for whom?

I gave birth acknowledging the responsibility I carried. I honored that responsibility but the fulfillment of that responsibility was mine to take on, not my child's.

I am beginning to feel as if I am running out of words, running out of angles, running out of…time. You were 75 when you died, Leslie. I am damn close to that age now. I'm likely going to take this to my grave.

But then, I've already made the plans to be cremated.

Chapter 21
Addressing The Sins
Of The Mothers

What is undergone psychologically is not easily explained. When I began questioning what had happened, when I began seeing holes in the fabric of the family tale being told, I sought to figure out what did happen. What I thought was a cut and dry, agreed upon history, began to unravel as I began to reexamine what facts were corroborated.

Questioning the tale, I was met with hostility. They expected me to move on just as they *believed* they had. I refused to participate in the façade. They attempted to cajole, bribe, threaten, berate. All was done without offering additional supporting information other than complaints regarding their relationships with others or, proclaiming their "love" of me as they alluded to their "imminent" deaths.

Much was learned about the relationship of Leslie and Lynnette. Much was learned about how, somehow, I had become the conduit between them. Perhaps it began with my naming. Perhaps it began when Lynnette taught me to write in all those years of correspondence between us. Perhaps I was purposely placed by Leslie to be the barrier, the buffer between herself and Lynnette. Whatever birthed my position, like with any structure, it must be maintained or it begins to not fulfill the purpose for which it was created in the first place. Then again, it can definitely be argued that

I was one definitely accidentally produced child. Much of our lives are accidentally created by lack of knowledge, wrong action, or ill-advised intent. We fool only ourselves when we state that it is passion that overcame us…nope, only fear.

These new insights came at the expense of the tale as told by Leslie. No other was protected by this misinformation. Leslie knew why she had earned my distrust but, she would not confront that knowledge. I believe that she would not confront that knowledge even to herself which is why it became, in time, to be her version, her TRUTH of what had happened.

A month after her death, in December of 2000, I would receive an email from Gary stating that he and Leslie never consulted with anyone other than the Chaplain. He also states he initiated the connection to that Chaplain.

Leslie had done nothing other than confront my abuser with Gary standing next to her. It was Gary that stood between me and any further sexual abuse. From what I would later learn, I suspect that her inaction, specifically remaining married, also allowed my abuser to continue to abuse her son. Mac never spoke up when that window of opportunity was opened in Germany. We know that there were repercussions to that silence.

Feelings of loss and emptiness may never completely go away. When she passed in 2000, I declared to my brother, a few days later, that I was not through with her yet. I said it in anger. I meant it. I mean it. What is obvious is not always what you want, but it is what you need to face.

I **want** to say I love my mother even unto and past the hate of the childhood I lost, the childhood potentials my brother lost, the opportunities she lost. Love, my love, anyone's love, does not excuse abuse. Love is not a salve to be placed on a festering wound, sealing it over so it may contaminate the body further. Love is a responsibility. Love does not absolve. Lost opportunity seldom finds its home after the door is shut.

As I gain in years, I wonder about whether it is Leslie I want to love or the possibility of what Leslie could have been in my life. There is the same confusion when it comes to my brother. Sam, as well as Leslie later on, had a lot to do with the separation of sister and brother. Our worlds physically no longer coincided when Gary and I married. We had both ceased to be concerned about the other long before. As to the two so-called fathers....

There does seem to be some nerve ending that has pain in relation to my genetic father. If you're not around, it's a bit difficult to do damage to a vague remembrance. As for the adoptive father, the Father-not-Father, I suspect what may have existed, if it ever existed at all, was not given enough nourishment to subsist. I suspect what might have been, died long before it was formed.

Gary.... That's taken a long time to undo in my psyche. Most of the grieving had long ago been faced after our second divorce. The betrayals rivaled Leslie's and when I consider the two offspring, my blood runs cold because of what he cost them. Even so, his death did not go unnoticed by my emotional system. It was brief, but it was present.

James, Sam, and Gary cost me a great deal—they cost me family. Specifically, they cost me the potential of my family. Each man eroded the economic base not only by not contributing to it but by actually draining what little resources that did exist. All three did nothing other than take whatever there was of value, devaluing what might have remained.

What I sought to address was addressed. What came of that process was not what I anticipated. Opportunities presented themselves but it would appear that the status quo was required by everyone but me. As a wise friend once told me: "You've gotta have something to work with."

In attempting to eradicate the damage done, I must somehow get across that although family is everything, it cannot be everything. While the family sustains us, it cannot contain us. When the family breaks its contract with one of its members, why is of paramount importance.

Family is what it allows each of its members to be. It cannot be the excuse for abuse. It cannot be that which you seek only in time of need. Family is a living entity. It is sustained by love and it is depleted by greed, and it suffers and gains by the totality of its members.

Chapter 22
Bessie And Opportunity

"...no matter what was said or done to remember the truth was within myself and I could keep all the trouble, but to be forgiving and not allow hatred and trouble grow within me."

18 Apr 97 letter, Bessie quote as remembered by her daughter, Lynnette.

That Bessie leaves us in 1952, making her unavailable to aid Lynnette and Leslie's relationship after I was born, is something of a personal travesty for me. It won't be until my early 30's, that I will begin to be aware of why the few times Bessie's name was uttered it reflected such a level of respect from the speaker.

My mother, Leslie Elizabeth, was named after her father and her maternal grandmother respectively. These two people were extraordinarily important in her life. Yet, for about half of my present life-span, there was little to no mention of the woman who passed just a year after my birth. My veil on Bessie was lifted in November of 1985.

During my first pregnancy in 1970, out of the seeming blue, I began to write. It wasn't my first time doing so, but it was pretty much the first time doing so without first being instructed by a teacher to do so. For some reason, the creative spigot got turned on and it was primarily in the form of poetry that the flow materialized.

Perhaps it was because I was finally out of the prison I'd been living in. Perhaps it was because much of my time was spent alone when Gary was working. Perhaps it was the chemical changes in my now pregnant body. Whatever it was that set me off, I was off and running. There just did not seem to be enough paper and pen in the world! Years down the road, I would share some of them with Grandmother. A poem, here and there, would just pop up in my part of our ritual writings.

August of 1985, around my 34th birthday, she began suggesting that I show a sampling of my poetry to someone she knew. Carolyn Lane was one of Lynnette's nieces, the daughter of her elder brother. Carolyn was also among those that Lynnette corresponded with on a regular basis. Lynnette mentioned my writings to Carolyn. Carolyn suggested that her husband, an English Professor, take a look at them.

I was spooked about the whole idea. Not having anticipated that Grandmother would share my poetry with anyone, I really was…okay, I was petrified! My psyche cried out: "Protect the Poetry!" Finally, I came to the realization that this was Grandmother asking, I needed to take it seriously, and that same psyche was also breathlessly going buttttttt whatttttt if it's good? So, in November of 1985 I sent a mailing to Professor Lane.

What followed continues to be one of the major highlights of my life for so many reasons. After reading my work he called. The phone conversation left me breathless. It left me so out of balance that I asked if he would mind writing down what he had told me because I wasn't quite certain I would remember. I felt so utterly over my head, astonished, although I don't believe I used that word in speaking with him. I was being told I was good at something; I was a natural at something. I was being likened to Bessie? Bessie was a writer? Bessie was a poet?

I received his letter shortly after our phone conversation. The letter is typed and goes on for about a page and a half. An excerpt from his letter states:

"I think I do neither of you an injustice in saying that it reminds me of your great-grandmother's work—the same kind of intellectual fire, the same kind of sensitive insights, the same aptness of metaphor. If there is anything to genetics, you certainly received her creativity in full measure. She would have been extremely proud of you and what you have written. The two of you would have gotten along famously."

Richard and Carolyn Lane knew Bessie as they were of my mother's generation. To be compared to the woman most revered by both Leslie and Lynnette remains for me, to this day, astonishing. But who was Bessie?

In March of 1879, my Great-Grandmother was born in Newton, Iowa. Her birth name was Caroline Elizabeth Anderson. She would be known as "Bessie." She was a school teacher in the very late 1800s in the county of Lincoln, in the state of Kansas. The 26th of April 1900, she married Arthur Jehu Stanley who was Lincoln County's Superintendent of Schools. Arthur Jehu Stanley, Sr. - Kansas Memory

There would be six children. The firstborn, Arthur Jr., would be born in 1901. Twins would be born in 1903. The girl, Juanita, would survive. Warren, would not make it to his first birthday. Their fourth child, Lynnette, would be born a year later in 1904. Elizabeth would arrive in 1909, followed four years later by Rose in 1913.

I remember being told by Lynnette that when her father decided to become a lawyer, he and her mother would study the law together. Her father would often boast that Bessie knew the law better than he and that it was not unusual for him to consult with her. By all accounts, the couple was close and very respectful of each other and their children.

In the year Lynnette was born, Bessie was urged by her sister, Rose, and her husband, Arthur to enter an essay contest that was sponsored by "The Brown Book Magazine." The topic of the essay was to be 100 words or less on what constituted "Success."

You've likely heard of "...live well, laugh often, and love much...." The full essay is as follows:

"He has achieved success who has lived well, laughed often and loved much; who has gained the respect of intelligent men, the trust of pure women and the love of little children; who has filled his niche and accomplished his task; who has left the world better than he found it; whether by an improved poppy, a perfect poem or a rescued soul; who has never lacked appreciation of earth's beauty or failed to express it; who has looked for the best in others and given them the best he had; whose life was an inspiration, whose memory is a benediction.*"[37] There are many variations to this essay that exist. The one listed here is from her tombstone.

I like to think that much of Bessie was reflected in Lynnette. Thinking this does give me comfort that there truly can be mother-daughter relationships that strengthen both.

One of the few remaining physical items I have of Leslie's is a gift she gave me a few years prior to our rift. I consider it a family memento and it is displayed in a wonderful, antique wooden cabinet that at one time belonged to one of my husband's Great Aunts. The cabinet contains quite a few things such as a marionette that Lynnette made in the early 1950's when William was still alive. She

---

[37] Bessie Anderson Stanley - Wikipedia

told me he created the set of wooden sticks, the controllers, to which the strings of the puppet are connected.

Lynnette was very industrious and very creative. When the kids and I returned to the Midwest from Virginia, descending on Leslie and she in Leavenworth, she purchased two twin beds and outfitted their room in Star Wars prints. From the linens she had found on sale she created curtains, upholstered a backless chair, set up their beds…all because she knew they were huge fans.

Aside from the dresses she made me from McCall's patterns when I was in my very early grade school years, she made a wedding dress for one of my cousins and a Confederate reenactment dress for Leslie. There were also the dolls. She outfitted one for each Presidential couple. I remember one that she made that was hemmed circle scraps sewn and then strung onto the head and limbs of the doll. The hands and feet had bells attached to them so that they made constant music when you played with them. The dolls head had "hair" constructed from an old stuffed animal. It was one of the many treasures lost over time, made by her hands.

Leslie was only creative by purposely seeming not to compete. Whatever Lynnette did she never attempted. Hence, she did not sew, she crocheted. She did not make dolls, she did calligraphy:

Opportunity

If only Bessie had lived a bit longer.

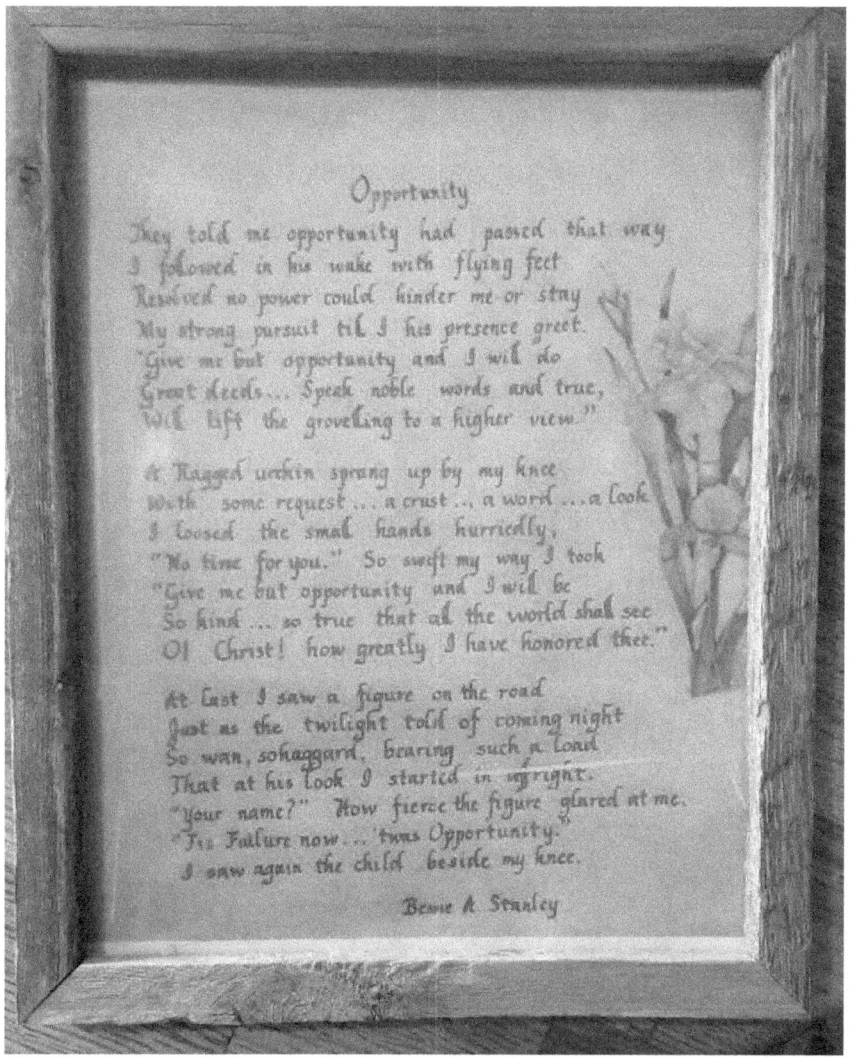

Opportunity

They told me opportunity had passed that way
I followed in his wake with flying feet
Resolved no power could hinder me or stay
My strong pursuit til I his presence greet.
"Give me but opportunity and I will do
Great deeds... Speak noble words and true,
Will lift the groveling to a higher view."

A Ragged urchin sprang up by my knee
With some request ... a crust ... a word ... a look
I loosed the small hands hurriedly,
"No time for you." So swift my way I took
"Give me but opportunity and I will be
So kind ... so true that all the world shall see
O! Christ! how greatly I have honored thee."

At last I saw a figure on the road
Just as the twilight told of coming night
So wan, so haggard, bearing such a load
That at his look I started in affright.
"Your name?" How fierce the figure glared at me.
"Fis Failure now ... 'twas Opportunity.'
I saw again the child beside my knee.

Bessie A. Stanley

Opportunity

"They told me opportunity had passed that way
I followed in his wake with flying feet
Resolved no power could hinder me or stay
My strong pursuit til his presence greet.
'Give me but opportunity and I will do
Great deeds.... Speak noble words and true,
Will lift the groveling to a higher view.'

A ragged urchin sprang up by my knee
With some request...a crust...a word...a look.
I loosed the small hands hurriedly,
'No time for you.' So swift my way I took.
'Give me but opportunity and I will be
So kind...so true that all the world shall see
O! Christ! How greatly I have honored thee.'

At last I saw a figure on the road
Just as the twilight told of coming night
So wane, so haggard, bearing such a load
That at his look I started in affright.

'Your name?' How fierce the figure glared at me.

'Tis Failure now…'twas Opportunity.'

I saw again the child beside my knee."

Bessie A. Stanley

Chapter 23
Closure

Family continues to be an issue. The travails of the adult continue. Even as I continue to grow, seeking answers, more questions appear. Perhaps you too have noticed how the more you learn, the more you increase your knowledge of this world, the more you know you don't know. I know I still have a lack of understanding, a lack of solid information, a lack of closure. Maybe there is no closure. Perhaps life is much like writing, much like what is said about poetry never being finished but simply abandoned. Sooner or later the script ends. I have no argument with the universe. It is what it is.

I've often stated, to my kids in particular, that drowning people should not help drowning people. The logic of that is obvious to most folks. When a drowning person attempts to save another drowning person, the odds are pretty high both are going down. Sometimes it can be pulled off. Sometimes perhaps you are not quite as down-trodden as you think you are and the save is made. A hero emerges and all applaud, all are strengthened by the willingness to risk all for another. This is certainly commendable. Just as certain is the pain felt when the attempt is made and both drown.

There is another aspect to this analogy and that is when the attempt to save a drowning person is made by someone who is unaware that they too are drowning. Sometimes when your reserves have been depleted over a long period of time, you've been tapped out for so long that you've been unaware that you are literally persisting on fumes. The tank has emptied because you just keep thinking, ah, I can get another mile, just one more mile.

There have been a few times I know I have run on fumes. I've been lucky in some ways and very unlucky in others. Not understanding you are drowning may not end your life but it can certainly contribute to loss within your life. As I've mentioned elsewhere in this missive, choices are made consequences follow.

The intention to do right is not always going to lead to right being done. The action has to be the right action, and that action is made with what is known, what is understood at the time of the action. Fairy Tale Heroes seldom complete the quest the first time, but they know to learn from the setbacks. When you sin, when you miss the target, check your intention and knowledge. Fairy Tales must be earned.

All That Is

The god I know needs my life to resolve our issues.
The god I know requires a fight—not for, not against, with.
The god I know created all that is about me.

All I know is all that is.

Despairs begin to surface, creating the reality I am to face.
In the end, comes a finite answer.
Always the dance precludes the grace.

No equation can produce so complete a picture.
No search of history can these moments be retraced.
The final answer, a custom-made moment, the god I know and I have made.

Astounded, we marvel in our deed!
Admonished, how our hearts do ache.
A mix of empathetic, joyous sorrow—all I know is the dance we've made.

The god I know is never silent.
I know we never rest.
In preparation, in anticipation, awaiting our next quest.